# LMS SHEDS
*in Camera*

# LMS
## SHEDS
### *in* *Camera*

**John Hooper**

**Oxford Publishing Co.**

Typesetting by:
Aquarius Typsetting Services, New Milton, Hants.

Printed in Great Britain by:
Netherwood Dalton & Co. Ltd., Huddersfield, Yorks.

Published by:
Oxford Publishing Co.
Link House
West Street
POOLE, Dorset

*Frontispiece:* One of the L&YR 4-4-2 locomotives
stands outside Low Moor Shed in 1905.
*J. H. Wright*

# Introduction

This book represents a photographic record of some of the engine sheds inherited by the London, Midland & Scottish Railway Company at the Grouping. In addition to the sheds, or motive power depots as the LMS titled them in the 1930s' reorganization and modernization scheme, included are photographs of the servicing facilities that served the railway companies prior to 1923 and, in some cases, passed into British Railways' days and also photographs of the locomotives that used them. The modernization carried out in earnest by the LMS, from 1933 onwards, to the dawn of nationalization, is represented by views of rebuilding and of new facilities, such as mechanical coal and ash plants, which brought, in return for the massive investment, greater efficiency to the motive power department. This enabled the Company to cut its locomotive fleet by a third and yet allow what remained to run greater mileages in revenue-earning service.

The last section of the book is devoted to views of the sheds after closure and shows the fate of some of them, most, of course, suffering the final indignity of demolition.

The steam motive power depot is now a memory, the like of which will never be seen again, although a dedicated band of enthusiasts and preservationists have revived some of the old magic at Carnforth ex-LMS Depot, where locomotives can be seen in steam and in various stages of repair and restoration, in the setting of a shed left just as British Railways vacated it, complete with the only remaining mechanical coaling plant in the country.

This book aims to capture some of the past glory of the steam age engine shed, and I hope that readers will get as much pleasure from its pages as I did in compiling the book.

Finally, I should like to express my sincere thanks to all the men behind the cameras and to those who so readily allowed me access to their photographic collections.

*John Hooper*
*1983*

Opened in October 1890, Mold Junction was a typical LNWR period shed complete with a 'northlight' roof. A standard coaling stage, with a water tank above, and a spacious yard with a 42 ft. turntable completed the facilities. The depot faired well in the LMS modernization scheme of the 1930s when a mechanical coaling plant with a 75 ton capacity bunker and a single skip ash disposal plant, from where this photograph was taken, were erected and brought into use in 1938. To cater for the larger freight types that appeared in the same period, a 60 ft. vacuum-operated turntable was installed in 1934. The depot's chief duty was to supply motive power for the freight traffic in the Chester area and in addition to the former LNWR 0-8-0s it had within its allocation, the shed also had a number of LMS-built locomotives on its books such as Stanier 2-6-0s, 4-6-0s and half a dozen 4F 0-6-0s, by the end of the LMS era. This view, taken in 1946, looking east towards Chester, shows the shed's position, beside Saltney Ferry Station. The 'Jinty' coming 'on shed' is No. 7656, one of seven such engines which were allocated to Mold Junction in 1946. Although the shed closed in April 1966, the shed building, rebuilt by British Railways, still stands and is in private use.

*Author's Collection*

# List of Engine Sheds

A copy of the original list of engine sheds, inherited by the London, Midland & Scottish Railway, that was drawn up at Derby in 1925. Although the list is not 100 per cent accurate, it does show that the men at Derby, who, at that time, thought that the Midland Railway ran the show, tried to keep an up to date list of the new Company's motive power establishments.

## London Midland and Scottish Railway Company.

## LIST OF ENGINE SHEDS.

| Name. | Designation | Main Depot. | Shed No. | Sorting Centre No. | Sub-depots. |
|---|---|---|---|---|---|
| **MIDLAND DIVISION.** | | | | | |
| Buckle, H. B. | DLS | Derby | 1 | | |
| Carey, E. K. | DLS | Carlisle | 33 | | |
| Rigby, T. A. E. | DLS | Skipton | 30 | | Lancaster, Hellifield, Ingleton. |
| Pegler, R. | DLS | Leeds | 28 | | Manningham, Keighley, Ilkley, Normanton & B., Stourton. |
| Moulang, F. D. | DLS | York & B. | 27 | | |
| Mc.Callum, P. | DLS | Sheffield & A. | 25 | | Millhouses, Canklow, Masboro'. |
| Rogerson, A. W. F. | DLS | Hasland | 23 | | Staveley, Sheepbridge, Westh'ses. |
| Slack, F. R. | DLS | Liverpool | 19 | | Walton, Widnes. |
| Slade, F. W. | DLS | Belle Vue | 21 | | Trafford Park, Heaton Mersey, Northwich. |
| Booth, E. L. | DLS | Buxton & A. | 20 | | Rowsley. |
| Donne, F. E. M. | DLS | Nottingham | 18 | | Mansfield, Kirkby, Lincoln, Southwell. |
| Kemp, F. | DLS | Toton | 17 | | |
| Harvey, R. F. | DLS | Burton-on-Trent & A. | 2 | | |
| Taylor, A. S. | DLS | Saltley | 3 | | Bournville, Redditch, Stratford-on-Avon, Blisworth. |
| Bevins, J. H. | DLS | Worcester | 4 | | Bromsgrove. |
| | DLS | Brecon | 5 | | |
| Jelley, R. | DLS | Upper Bank | 6 | | Gurnos. |
| Peet, W. G. | DLS | Bristol | 8 | | Glo'ster, Evesham, Tewkesb'y, Bath, Dursley, Ashchurch, Thornbury. |
| Shaw, F. T. | DLS | Peterboro' & A. | 9 | | Bourne. |
| Fox, R. H. | DLS | Leicester | 10 | | Coalville, Stockingford, Wigston. |
| Anker, F. C. | DLS | Wellingboro' | 13 | | Kettering, Cambridge. |
| Stevens, W. I. | DLS | Bedford & A. | 14 | | |
| Talbot, E. E. A. | DLS | Kentish Town | 16 | | Cricklewood, St. Albans. |
| Abraham, F. W. | DLS | Plaistow | — | | Upminster, Tilbury, Shoeburyness. |
| **WESTERN "A" DIVISION.** | | | | | |
| Wicken, J. | DLS | Devons Road | — | 1 A | |
| Firbank, G. J. L. | DLS | Willesden | 2 | 2 | Watford. |
| Dibb, W. H. | RSF | Bletchley | 3 | 3 | Leighton, Cambridge, Banbury, Oxford, Aylesbury, Newport Pagnell. |
| Bostock. H K / ~~Nevitt, J. H.~~ | RSF | Camden | 1 | 1 A | |
| Austin, H. | DLS | Rugby | 8 | 5 | Warwick, Coventry, Market Harboro', Stamford, Seaton. |
| Nightingale, J. | RSF | Northampton | 5 | 4 | |
| | | N. & Colwick | 7 | 4 | |
| Alcock, T. C. | RSF | Nuneaton | 4 | 8 | Coalville, Leicester, Loughboro' Overseal. |
| Waddington, J. W. | DLS | Walsall & M. | 9 | 7 | Dudley, Hednesford. |
| | | Bescot | 6 | 6 | |
| Firkin, A. E. | DLS | Aston | 10 | 6 | Monument Lane. |
| Longstaff, J. W. | RSF | Bushbury | 13 | 7 | |
| Bolderston, A. E. | DLS | Crewe | 15 | 13 | Whitchurch. |
| Howard, T. P. L. | RSF | Stafford | 14 | 9 | |
| Clews, R. T. | DLS | Shrewsbury | 30 | 10 | Ludlow, Coalport, Craven Arms, Clee Hill, Builth Rd., Knighton. |
| Cheetwood, T. | DLS | Longsight | 16 | 17 | Stockport, Lees, Altrincham. |
| Thomasson, J. E. | DLS | Springs Branch | 25 | 24 | |
| Winby, C. E. | RSF | Sutton Oak | 24 | 23 | |
| Turnbull, Richard | RSF | Warrington | 23 | 22 | Arpley, Over & Wharton. |
| Davies, W. H. | DLS | Edge Hill | 26 | 23 | |
| Lloyd, J. | RSF | Speke Junction | 35 | 23 | Widnes. |
| Whitehead, T. F. | DLS | Preston | 27 | 25 | Lancaster, Garstang. |
| Blakesley, W. E. | RSF | Carnforth & M. | | | |
| Nelson, G. H. | DLS | Carlisle | 29 | 27 | Penrith, Maryport. |
| Turnbull, Ralph | RSF | Tebay | 28 | 30 | Oxenholme, Ingleton. |
| Power, W. H. | DLS | Abergavenny | 31 | 11 | Hereford & M., Tredegar, Bl'navon. |
| Rowbottom, J. | RSF | Swansea | 33 | 12 | Carmarthen, Llandovery. |
| O'Hara, D. | DLS | Patricroft | 34 | 19 | Plodder Lane. |
| Needham, J. | RSF | Farnley Junction | 17 | 20 | |
| Ward, W. G. | RSF | Huddersfield | 20 | 20 | |
| Whitmill, C. | DLS | Llandudno Jct. | 38 | 14 | Blaenau Festiniog, Denbigh, Rhyl, Corwen. |
| Dingley A / ~~Bostock, H. K.~~ | RSF | Bangor | 21 | 15 | Carnarvon, Amlwch. |
| Mercer, I. E. | RSF | Holyhead | 22 | 16 | |
| Frost, G. A. | DLS | Chester | 19 | 14 | |
| Dovey, E. | RSF | Birkenhead | 18 | 14 | Hooton, Ellesmere Port. |
| Martlew, R. | RSF | ,, Docks | — | 14 | |
| Blake, G. E. H. | RSF | Mold Junction | 37 | 14 | |
| Longsdale, T. H. | Ass't. Supt. | Stoke, N.S. | — | — | Macclesfield, Alsager, Leek Brook, Market Drayton, Caldon Quarry, Ashb'rne, Uttoxeter, Hulme End. |
| Sharples, E. | Ass't. Supt. | Barrow (Furness) | — | — | Moor Row, Lakeside, Coniston. |
| Burgess, J.F. / ~~Collin, T.~~ | RSF | Workington | 32 | 30 | |
| Nightingale, J. | RSF | Greenore | — | — | |
| **WESTERN "B" DIVISION.** | | | | | |
| Tetlow, E. I. | DLS | Newton Heath | 1 | 40 | |
| Mason, E. | RSF | Agecroft | 13 | 40 | |
| Shawcross, W. Y. | DLS | Low Moor | 2 | 52 | |
| Muff, S. | RSF | Sowerby Bridge | 3 | 50 | |
| Bourne, E. C. | RSF | Mirfield | 5 | 53 | |
| Elliott, J. S. | DLS | Wakefield | 6 | 54 | Barnsley, Hull. |
| Schofield, H. | RSF | Goole | 10 | 54 | Knottingley, Doncaster. |
| Grafton, W. C. | DLS | Bolton | 14 | 41 | |
| Burge, J. F. | RSF | Wigan | 16 | 24 | |
| Hurst, J. | RSF | Horwich | 15 | 40 | |
| Warren, R. A. | DLS | Bank Hall | 18 | 43 | |
| Sangster, W. M. | RSF | Southport | 17 | 44 | |
| Davenport, J. | RSF | Aintree | 19 | 43 | |
| Ludwig, A. C. | RSF | Ormskirk | 29 | 43 | |
| Shortt, H. G. | DLS | Bury | 20 | 40 | |
| Grafton, T. H. | RSF | Bacup | 21 | 40 | |
| Moore, F. G. | DLS | Accrington | 22 | 46 | |
| Wilding, R. C. | RSF | Rose Grove | 23 | 46 | |
| Crompton, J. H. | RSF | Colne | 24 | 40 | |
| Clayton, F. T. | RSF | Lower Darwen | 25 | 41 | |
| Morgan, H. J. | RSF | Hellifield | 26 | 45 | |
| Sheridan, J. J. P. | DLS | Blackpool | 32 | 25 | Blackpool T.R. 31. |
| Jarrett, A. H. | RSF | Fleetwood | 30 | 55 | |
| Turner, J. E. | RSF | Lostock Hall | 27 | 25 | |
| **NORTHERN DIVISION.** | | | | | |
| Davidson, W. | DLF | Aberdeen | | | |
| White, J. C. | DLF | Beattock | | | Lockerbie, Leadhills. |
| Hynd, S. W. | DLF | Kingmoor | | | Kirtlebridge. |
| | DLF | Carstairs | | | |
| Dale, T. | DLF | Dawsholm | | | Airdrie, Dumbarton, Yoker. |
| Pool, S. | DLF | Dundee | | | Blairgowrie. |
| Grafton, A. T. | DLF | Edinburgh | | | |
| Spence, W. | DLF | Forfar | | | Alyth, Arbroath, Brechin, Montrose. |
| MacDonald, A. | DLF | Gr'nock (Ladyb'n) | | | Wemyss Bay. |
| Prentice, H. G. | DLF | Motherwell | | | Grangemouth, Greenhill, Hamilton, Strathaven. |
| Hutchison, R. | DLF | Oban | | | Ballachulish. |
| Dalziel, W. | DLF | Perth (South) | | | Balquhidder, Crieff, Methven. |
| Keyden, J. | DLF | Polmadie | | | Ardrossan (North), Irvine, Govan, Kilbirnie, Paisley (St. James), Baillieston. |
| Liddell, J. | DLF | St. Rollox | | | |
| Brown, A. | DLF | Stirling | | | Callender, Denny, Killin. |
| Hannah, H. | DLF | Ardrossan | | | Fairlie Pier. |
| Dowie, J. | DLF | Newton on Ayr | | | Dallmellington. |
| Cochrane, J. | DLF | Corkerhill | | | |
| Bradshaw, J. | DLF | Dumfries | | | Kirkcudbright. |
| Mc.Connachie, G. | DLF | Girvan | | | |
| Baker, E. | DLF | Greenock (Princes Pier) | | | |
| Lyon, D. | DLF | Hurlford | | | Beith. |
| Middleton, J. | RSF | Troon Harbour | | | |
| Caldwell, T. | DLF | Muirkirk | | | |
| White, R. | DLF | St. Enoch | | | |
| Martin, J. | DLF | Stranraer | | | Newton Stewart, Millisle. |
| Smith, J. | DLF | Inverness | | | Dingwall, Tain, Dornoch, Fort George, Fortrose. |
| Henderson, P. | RSF | Wick | | | Lybster, Thurso. |
| Tewsley, H. | RSF | Helmsdale | | | |
| Ross, D. A. | RSF | Kyle of Lochalsh | | | |
| Mc.Kenzie, J. | RSF | Forres | | | Keith, Burghead, Fochabers. |
| Gault, W. | RSF | Aviemore | | | Kingussie. |
| Nisbet, J. | DLF | Perth (North) | | | Aberfeldy. |
| Bain, W. | RSF | Blairatholl | | | |

DLS—District Locomotive Superintendent.    RSF—Running Shed Foreman.    DLF—District Locomotive Foreman.

M.—Midland Division, A.—"A" Division, B.—"B" Division, N.—Northern Division.

**CHIEF GENERAL SUPERINTENDENT.**

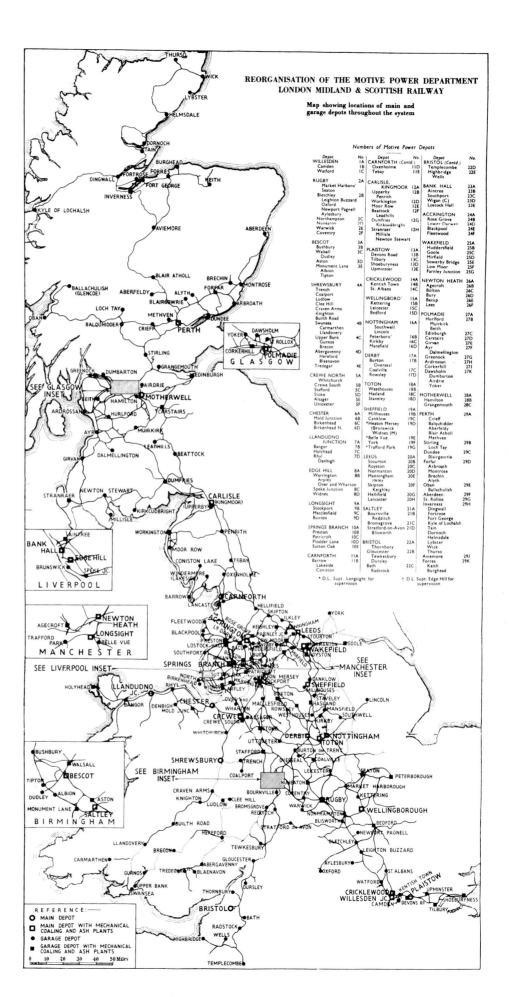

A map of the LMS motive power depots, in 1935, which was the middle age period of that great railway company. The shed code was the first universal code created by the Company but the depots still came under one of four divisions: the Central Division, covering the old L&YR area; the Midland Division, covering the MR area; the Western Division, covering the ex-LNWR and the whole of Scotland which came under the Northern Division.

# NEW AND REBUILT SHEDS

*Plate 1:*   Crewe South, in December 1896, only weeks before the shed was occupied by the Running Department. The construction was of typical London & North Western Railway design with a 'northlight' roof, and with offices running along the side of the building. This type of shed design, introduced by Webb, was cheap and quick to erect when compared with the earlier hipped roof engine sheds used by the Company, but, as was shown in later years, it was prone to accelerated deterioration when compared with the more robust hipped roof sheds. The Lancashire & Yorkshire Railway also employed the 'northlight' design for many of their engine sheds but other constituent companies of the LMS used the 'northlights' at only a few sites, and some, not at all. It fell to the LMS to rebuild the engine shed roofs which it had inherited and the majority in need of rebuilding were originally fitted with 'northlights'.

*National Railway Museum*

*Plate 2:*   An interior view of the completed shed at Crewe South.
*A. G. Ellis*

*Plate 3:* The new Caledonian Railway engine shed at Grangemouth Fouldubs, in 1900, not long after it opened, with a recently delivered 812 class 0-6-0 locomotive No. 859 (later 17597) on the right-hand road. This standard Caledonian shed design incorporated transversed pitched roofs over the stabling roads and a front to back single pitch roof over the No. 1 repair road. The repair shop was equipped with a 40 ton engine hoist, and a 30,000 gallon water tank was perched on top at the rear of the shop. A 70 ft. turntable was supplied and the coaling stage was of the usual single road timber type that was popular with this Company. The depot had replaced a previous shed, dating from the 1860s, and at the Grouping, had twenty five locomotives allocated consisting mainly of 0-6-0 tender and 0-6-0 tank engines. In December 1947, Stanier 8Fs, Nos. 8147—52 were allocated to this shed together with twenty seven ex-Caledonian engines. Crabs, No. 2736/7 and 4Fs Nos. 3883 and 4320 were also based here. The depot closed to steam in October 1965 and is today used as a diesel depot.

*National Railway Museum*

*Plate 4:* In the 1940s, the LMS employed concrete in precast sections for much of its rebuilding and new building programmes. The sections used were of a standard size and shape and would fit in at most sites chosen. This method and material helped to keep costs down and speeded up the work due to be undertaken. The majority of the concrete sections were cast at Newton Heath Concrete Works where this kind of work is still in full swing today. This view shows the ex-MR shed at Lincoln undergoing a complete rebuild in the latter part of World War II.

*Author's Collection*

*Plates 5 & 6:* Further examples of LMS shed rebuilding are these two views of Aintree, in October 1944, with the work nearly completed and Aston, with a close up of the various precast concrete segments. The view of Aston, taken in May 1944, shows work in the early stages with only four roads covered, and the patent glazing yet to be fitted. Behind, can be seen the enginemen's barracks which had a total of forty two beds.

*V. R. Anderson Collection*

Plates 7 & 8: The modernization of the ex-MR engine shed at Leicester was started in 1944, when a large concrete roundhouse was built to replace the two small and ancient mid-nineteenth century round sheds. Once the site was prepared, preformed sections were joined together and these views show the methods and type of construction employed. The new shed was ready for use by late 1945, but the modernization of the whole of the depot's facilities was not completed until nine years later. One other roundhouse of this type was built, by the LMS, at Carlisle Upperby.

*British Rail*

*Plate 9:* Newton Heath was the largest shed on the ex-L&YR with twenty stabling roads under cover and four roads leading into the repair shop, and it fell to the LMS to re-roof the stabling shed in 1935/6. This view, taken in 1936, shows the last four roads receiving the new 'single pitch' style roof. To the right can be seen the repair shop retaining the original hipped roof. Other improvements carried out at 26A, during the 1930s, were coaling plant, ash plants and the installation of a 70 ft. vacuum-operated turntable, as well as yard extensions at the east end of the shed.

*British Rail*

*Plate 10:* Rhyl Shed, in the early 1940s, during the re-roofing of the small three road establishment. Like many rebuilds on the LMS, the original walls were retained and a new roof was built and, in this case, the precast concrete beam and patent glazing method was employed. The original roof had been a pitched affair dating from the opening of the shed in 1870.

*J. M. Dunn*

*Plate 11:* This portion of the straight shed at Stoke had been without a roof since 1935 but, as this view shows, a start had been made, by the summer of 1938, to rebuild the whole shed. Even during the actual building, space was at such a premium at this depot that locomotives were stabled under the steel erectors' noses. On the left, the unusual ash plant, which actually lifted the narrow gauge skips out of the pits and transported them for tipping, is noteworthy.

*A. G. Ellis*

*Plates 12 & 13:* These two views of Skipton Shed show the massive rebuilding undertaken by British Railways in 1952. Prior to this, the two staggered sheds had been timber-built by the Midland Railway. The first, served by a 60ft. turntable, was erected in the late 1870s and the shed near to the main line was added in 1892. Building materials used for the new construction can be clearly seen with old rails making up the framework for the roof. The turntable had been installed by the LMS in 1938 and was fitted with a vacuum tractor. Before this date, a 46ft. turntable was all that was available and this was sited at the south end of the station. A standard MR coaling stage, built in 1892, served the depot until closure, in April 1967, after which the shed buildings were taken over by the local council to be used as a depot for refuge vehicles.

*British Rail*

*Plate 14:* The rebuilding of the roof at the ex-LNWR shed at Bletchley took place in 1954, and the materials employed by British Railways consisted of steel rails and troughing, and patent glazing, which was usual for the period. Although it was termed 'lightweight construction' one wonders just how long this type of roof would have lasted had steam power still been with us.

*British Rail*

# SERVICING FACILITIES

*Plate 15:* Toton coaling stage, on 10th December 1929. This standard Midland Railway double coaling stage had been built in 1900 to meet the requirements of depot expansion during that period. Coal was brought into the stage in wagons, via the ramp, and it was then transferred by hand into specially made metal tubs, seen hanging over the side of the stage, which, when full, were pushed on to one of two counterbalanced tipping frames. The coal was then discharged into the waiting locomotive tender on the road below. Shortly after this photograph was taken, the stage was demolished and replaced by a mechanical coaling plant. Two ash disposal plants were also erected to speed up the servicing procedure at this busy depot.

*National Railway Museum*

*Plate 16:* The enclosed all timber construction of a typical Glasgow & South Western Railway coaling stage, gave plenty of shelter from the elements for the coalmen at Ayr Depot.

*R. Barr*

*Plate 17:* The ex-Midland Railway engine shed at Upper Bank, near Swansea, did not warrant a standard type of coaling stage so, instead, this elevated coaling road, with a small shelter, was provided when the shed opened in 1893. However, by 1903, this more permanent all over structure was provided, lasting through the years with occasional recladding, until closure of the depot in February 1963.

*H. C. Casserley*

*Plate 18:* At Rugby, in 1885, the London & North Western Railway built this double width coaling stage. Only one half of the stage was topped with the usual water tank, the other half having two hipped roofs. Coal was tipped into locomotive tenders using 1 ton capacity wheeled tubs, which were pushed on to counterbalanced tipping platforms, seen here in the closed position, similar to the Midland Railway method. A few years after this 1930s' scene was captured, the stage was replaced by a 300 ton capacity mechanical coaling plant.

*H. C. Casserley Collection*

*Plate 19:* The Edge Hill coaling plant was unique, it being the only one of its type in this country. Built, in 1914, by the LNWR, and having three 40 ton capacity bunkers, this step towards semi-mechanization was used for a period of 54 years until closure of the depot to steam locomotives. Wagons were hoisted up the ramp by capstan and rope and when they had discharged their contents into the bunkers below, they were allowed to roll, by gravity, down to the empty siding. For this one plant, the company constructed 150 special bottom discharge wagons and in the photograph can be seen one of the original wagons running down to the empty line, whilst a Stanier 2-8-0 locomotive stands beneath one of the bunker discharge chutes.

*W. D. Cooper*

*Plate 20:* Polmadie was the first LMS depot in Scotland to receive a mechanical coaling plant, and this huge steel structure, erected in 1925, had two 150 ton bunkers which were separated by a centre 20 ton wagon hoist. Wagons were lifted to the top of the bunkers and tipped on end, the coal being discharged through the end door. A wagon turntable, seen just in front of the plant, enabled the operator to choose the bunker into which the wagon would tip. The plant was superseded, in 1946, by a new concrete coaling plant sited at the southern end of the depot yard.

*British Rail*

*Plate 21:* Ex-Caledonian Railway 'Jumbo', No. 17446 has its tender replenished at Polmadie's coaler in September 1934.

*W. L. Good*

*Plate 22:* Provided in 1893 to serve the new engine shed at Wakefield, the L&YR saw fit to build this double length standard coal stage with a water tank on top, but in 1930, a large 200 ton capacity mechanical coaling plant was erected, rendering this manual stage redundant. However, it was kept on for emergencies, such as the new plant breaking down and the water tank was also used for storage of the depot's supply. This July 1964 view clearly shows its likeness to the LNWR standard coaling stage.

*R. J. Essery*

Plate 23: The No. 1 size coaling plant at Kentish Town Motive Power Depot, in May 1941, shortly after it was brought into use. This structure contained two 150 ton storage bunkers which fed four discharge chutes. With this type of plant, coal was hoisted in a large 20 ton capacity skip, up to the bunkers where it was tipped. In this view, we see a wagon discharging its contents into the skip. One man could carry out all the operations required to get the coal into locomotive tenders and bunkers in a matter of minutes, and when one considers how labour intensive and slow the old manual coaling stages were, it was obviously worth the capital expenditure on such machinery at busy depots.

*British Rail*

*Plate 25:* Un-named 'Jubilee' class locomotive No. 5557, later to be named *New Brunswick*, positions its tender under the Preston coaling plant on a summer's day in 1936. The plant's discharge chutes are positioned on the side to suit the site, but it was usual to position them over the track, directly beneath the plant.

W. L. Good

*Plate 26:* One of the least-noticed pieces of equipment at motive power depots, as far as railway enthusiasts and modellers were concerned, was the coal drencher unit. This simple, yet quite effective appliance was used to soak the coal, in loaded wagons, with water, as the wagons passed along to the coaling plant, and so prevent clouds of coal dust being expelled as the wagons tipped their contents into the bunkers, which were situated 50 ft. above the ground. In the down position, shown here, the gantry automatically unleashed a deluge of water on to the coal and when out of use the counterweights lifted the gantry clear of the track.

*Author's Collection*

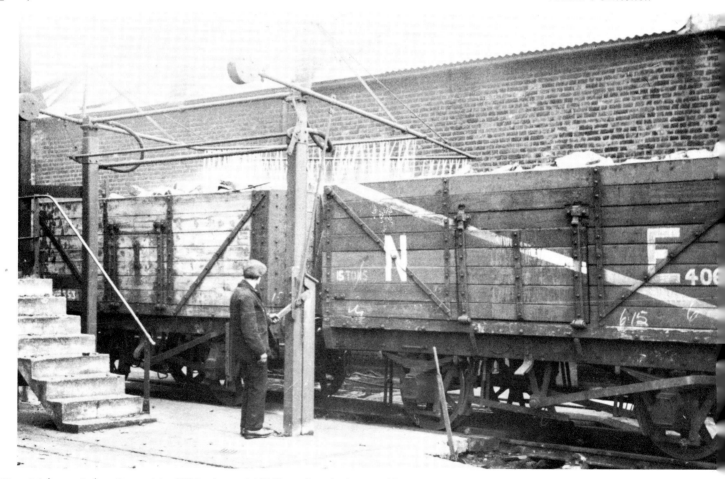

◄*Plate 24 (opposite):* Opened in 1883, the ex-LNWR engine shed at Bushbury was served by a standard type coaling stage with a tank above, but during the LMS modernization scheme in the 1930s, this No. 2 size coaling plant, with twin 75 ton capacity bunkers, was erected along with an ash plant. These No. 2 size plants were replenished by means of a wagon hoist which lifted the wagon bodily to a point above the bunkers, and then tipped it on its side to discharge its contents. In this 1941 official photograph, the large amount of coal dust that decorated the sides of the plant and, usually, the local neighbourhood, can be seen. In front of the plant is a drencher unit that helped to combat the dust nuisance.

*British Rail*

◄*Plate 27 (opposite):* A wagon load of Welsh coal is about to be hoisted and tipped into the Shoeburyness coaling plant. This style of plant was a one off design and was erected in the early 1930s as part of a £750,000 modernization scheme on the entire London, Tilbury & Southend line, when, at the same time, the engine shed at this location was extended from two roads to four.

British Rail

*Plate 28:* This official photograph, of Cricklewood coaling plant, taken in May 1931, shows the procedure for coaling locomotives with this type of plant. On the right the wagon tippler, emptying a load of coal into the underground bunker, can be seen, and half way up the right-hand side of the plant is the skip, transporting coal up to the storage bunker that was built into the structure. From this bunker, the coal was automatically drawn off for weighting and loading into tenders. Beyer-Garratt 2-6-6-2 No. 4977 was chosen to pose for the camera on this occasion, but it was not as clean as would be expected for an 'official'. In the background can be seen the two roundhouses of this ex-Midland Railway depot.

British Rail

*Plate 29:* The tippler and bucket conveyor type of coaling plant, installed by the LMS in 1931, at Wellingborough ex-Midland Railway engine shed. This type of unit was very similar to the two which were introduced by the London & North Western Railway at Camden and Carlisle Upperby prior to the Grouping. The LMS erected, also in 1931, a very similar plant at the new motive power depot built at Royston.

*British Rail*

*Plate 30:* Farnley Junction was the ex-LNWR engine shed at Leeds. Opened in 1882, the depot became part of the Central Division of the LMS in 1931, and qualified for modernization in the 1930s scheme, mainly due to the time it was taking to get locomotives through the servicing procedure. One of the improvements carried out included this single skip ash disposal plant, seen here tipping a load of ash into a waiting wagon. These plants lifted ashes and clinker from under-track grids, where ash previously dropped from fireboxes etc., into narrow gauge tubs, was tipped into a waiting skip. This skip was then hoisted by an electric motor to the discharge point above the waiting wagon.

*R. J. Essery*

*Plate 31:* The double skip girder type ash disposal plant at Wakefield Motive Power Depot, in the 1930s, with ex-L & YR locomotives, 0-8-0 No. 12871 and 2-4-2T No. 10953, making use of the facilities. In the background can be seen the huge coaling plant.

*National Railway Museum*

*Plate 32:* The new coaling and ash disposal plants, as yet without any ancillary machinery, stand, like threatening concrete monsters, at Crewe North Motive Power Depot, in April 1950. On the right is the black shape of what was the first mechanical coaling plant used in this country. This all steel structure, with its 270 ton capacity bunker, was brought into use in 1913 by the LNWR after being built to a design of Bowen-Cooke, in conjunction with the construction company of Babcock & Wilcox and was about to be superseded by the more modern machinery.

*H. C. Casserley Collection*

*Plate 34:* One year later, viewed from the other side of the yard, the new Crewe North No. 2 size coaling plant and ash disposal plants are in use, and the original plant is being dismantled. In the plans, drawn up by the LMS and later by British Railways, Crewe North was to have had two coaling plants and four ash plants serving two new roundhouses, but as it eventually turned out, only this set of plants was found to be necessary after the roundhouse schemes were dropped.

*British Rail*

*Plate 35:* Stanier Pacific No. 46228 *Duchess of Rutland* takes on water at Perth Motive Power Depot in 1961.

*G. B. McArthur*

*Plate 33 (opposite):* The ferro-concrete ash plant had very similar below ground level gear to the girder structures, but above ground they were different in that they could store up to 25 tons of ash in a bunker to await removal, by wagon, when full. This type of plant enabled the road beneath to be used as an ash pit and so save space; a facility much sought after at many installations. In this view, we see the Carnforth plant, in May 1941, not long after it was commissioned. Worthy of note are the two types of narrow gauge cars associated with these ash disposal plants.

*British Rail*

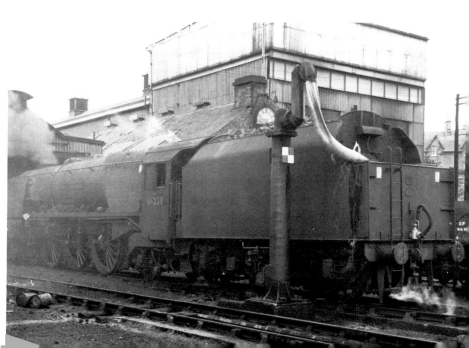

*Plate 36:* Ex-LNWR 'Cauliflower' 0-6-0 No. 8592 refills its tender from the tank on top of the coaling stage at Bescot in 1931. Many of these overhead tanks were used long after the coaling of locomotives had been passed over to mechanical plants.

*G. Coltas*

The next three photographs show the methods implemented by the Lancashire & Yorkshire Railway during the dry summers of 1910 through to 1914, when the Fylde coast was hit by drought, and the two Blackpool engine sheds, Central and Talbot Road, needed to have water transported in from the inland sheds, using spare locomotive tenders as the ideal mode.

*Plate 37:* Aspinall 0-6-0 No. 1030 (LMS No. 12093), of Rose Grove, waits, at the head of a train of tenders being loaded with water at Lostock Hall Shed, for movement to Blackpool on 30th September 1913.

*National Railway Museum*

*Plate 38:* This view of Blackpool Talbot Road, in 1913, later known as Blackpool North, shows two methods of transferring water from the supply tenders into locomotive tenders. On the top tender can be seen a hand pump and trough, whilst gravity was used to fill the trough leading out from between the two tenders on the coaling ramp. Both tenders, used singly or together, were slow, but simple and effective. *National Railway Museum*

*Plate 39:* A vacuum pump, set up next to a parachute tank at Blackpool Talbot Road, was the ultimate method of dealing with water transfer. Aspinall 2-4-2T No. 698 is creating the vacuum, as water is allowed, by gravity, to fill the below ground level tank and the water is then pumped up to fill the overhead tank. *National Railway Museum*

# BREAKDOWN TRAINS AND CRANES

The breakdown train is an important piece of machinery of any railway system and must be ready for immediate use if the system is to continue working efficiently. The LMS was no exception to the rule and, throughout the whole of the LMS, breakdown trains were kept at strategic engine sheds where it fell to the fitters and shed staff to man them. The majority of breakdown trains had a crane in their make-up, some being hand operated, having been inherited from the pre-grouping companies, but most cranes on the LMS inventory were steam-powered in 1941. The wheel arrangement, used in the captions which follow, is expressed in Whyte's notation, that is with the jib leading and laid on a match truck. In addition to the crane, tool vans, packing vans and travelling vans made up the breakdown train, these vans usually being retired goods and passenger vehicles.

*Plate 40:*   Although this view is not taken at an engine shed, it is included to show the breakdown gang, who were shed staff, at work re-railing a MR 0-6-4T, No. 2015. Saltley crane, No. 26, a 15 tonner supplied by Cowans Sheldon in 1893, is given a hand by the Derby breakdown crane, No. 249, a 40 ton capacity crane supplied to the Midland Railway in 1916 by Ransomes & Rapier. The incident depicted took place at King's Norton c 1922.

*W. L. Good*

*Plate 41:* The L&YR breakdown train at Low Moor Shed, in 1905, comprised the following vehicles: travelling van, 20 ton capacity hand crane, safety (match) wagon, packing van and a tool van. The Barton Wright 0-6-0 was No. 946 which became LMS No. 12033.                                                                                    *Author's Collection*

*Plate 42:* Craven Brothers of Reddish, Stockport, supplied steam breakdown cranes to many pre-grouping companies, and the LMS carried on that trend, in 1931, when it purchased two 36 ton capacity cranes. As it turned out, these were the only cranes supplied to the LMS by Cravens and this monster 4-8-4, with its detachable relieving bogies, was sent to Rugby Motive Power Depot. Initially numbered MP8, it was renumbered RS1013/50 in 1941, after being uprated, in 1939, to 50 tons capacity.                                                                                              *P. Tatlow Collection*

*Plate 43:*   Old meets new at Newton Heath in 1931. The ex-L&YR 20 ton crane on the left, supplied by Cowans Sheldon in 1902, meets the new LMS 36 ton steam crane, which had recently been delivered from nearby Craven Brothers. In the right foreground can be seen the fixed standpipe by which the crane would normally be stood, and connected to, whilst on shed. The Cowans Sheldon crane became No. MP28 soon after this photograph was taken and the Cravens unit became MP9. They were renumbered RS1062/20 and RS1015/50 respectively, in 1941, the Cravens crane having been uprated to 50 tons capacity.

*P. Tatlow Collection*

*Plate 44:*   One of the standard 0-6-4 steam cranes, rated at 30 tons, purchased by the LMS in 1942/3, from Ransomes & Rapier Ltd., of Ipswich. The five units Nos. RS1067–71 were initially sent to sheds in England, this particular crane going to Wellingborough in June 1942.

*British Railways*

*Plate 45:* This steam breakdown crane was allocated to Wakefield Shed in March 1925, and was resident until February 1943, when it went to Accrington. The unit was built for the Midland Railway in 1899 by Cowans Sheldon and was rated at 15 tons capacity. At the Grouping, the crane was stationed at Leeds Holbeck and was numbered MR30. Its LMS numbers were MP41 and RS1028/15.

*P. Tatlow Collection*

*Plate 46:* The Crewe North breakdown train, just before the Grouping. The crane had been purchased by the LNWR, in 1909, from from the makers Ransomes & Rapier. Rated at 36 ton capacity, the crane passed into LMS ownership and was numbered MP7, being again renumbered in the 1941 scheme to RS1012/36. In 1939, this unit was re-allocated to Newton Heath whilst Crewe North inherited an uprated 50 ton Cowans Sheldon crane from Leeds Holbeck.

*National Railway Museum*

# THE ENGINE SHEDS

*Plate 47:* Aberdeen Ferryhill, in the 1930s, with an assortment of LMS and LNER locomotives on shed. The Caledonian Railway brought this depot into use in 1908 and, after much wrangling over costs etc., agreed to rent four of the ten roads to the North British Railway in addition to supplying them with coal, water and sand, etc. The new shed was of a Caledonian design, with transverse roof pitches and a two road repair shop, fitted with a 30 ton capacity engine hoist. Next to the repair shop was a 70ft. turntable and beyond that, a double discharge coaling stage. After the Grouping, the LNER carried on with the agreement even though they had the use of the ex-Great North of Scotland shed at Kittybrewster. By 1950, there were only eight former LMS locomotives allocated to Ferryhill as opposed to thirty ex-LNER types. The 1935 code was 29F changing, in 1941, to 29B. British Railways recoded the depot, in January 1949, to 61B. The shed closed to steam in February 1967 and was one of the last in Scotland to deal with main line passenger locomotives.

*Real Photographs*

*Plate 48:* Agecroft, at the Grouping, with an unidentified Atlantic, probably No. 1418, moving off from the coaling road. The smoke haze, that was forever a feature of steam motive power depots, is very evident. The depot here was opened in 1889 to replace an engine shed at Hope Street, Salford. At the Grouping, 93 locomotives were allocated to this shed, including Atlantic No. 1418, but during the early 1930s, the allocation had dropped to the 50—60 mark remaining at around those figures until closure. The depot was responsible for a number of passenger workings out of the west side of Manchester Victoria, but the main reason for its existence was to look after a large freight locomotive stud working from the surrounding Brindle Heath Yards and Manchester Docks.

*National Railway Museum*

*Plate 49:* In this mid-1930s view of Agecroft, there is a predominance of ex-L&YR locomotives on shed, but the LMS standard types were infiltrating in ever increasing numbers. The original shed roof had been recently felted but the smoke vents had disappeared. By 1938, the LMS had provided a new 'single pitch' type roof but as it turned out, only the four roads nearest the new office extension received the new cover, the other four roads being left open to the elements right up to closure of the depot on 22nd October 1966.

*C. A. Appleton*

*Plate 50:* Probably Agecroft's most distinguished visitors assembled in the yard in September 1930. The occasion was a railway exhibition held at Manchester Victoria Station, as part of the centenary celebrations of the Liverpool & Manchester Railway, and these representatives from the 'Big Four' were assembled here ready for the short journey to Victoria Station. From left to right the locomotives are, LNER 4-6-4 No. 10000, GWR 4-6-0, *King Stephen*, LMS Beyer-Garratt No. 4972 and SR 4-6-0, *Lord Nelson*. The latter was, in fact, *Anson* masquerading as the class leader.

*C. A. Appleton Collection*

*Plate 51:* A general view of the ex-L&YR depot at Aintree, just after the Grouping. The shed had a 'northlight' roof and the coaling stage was of standard Company design. The 50ft. electric turntable was replaced, in 1936, by a 70ft. unit resited on the south side of the shed.

*National Railway Museum*

*Plate 52:* A view of Aintree on 4th June 1967, eight days before the depot closed. The coaling plant was erected in 1936/7 along with an ash plant, and the shed roof was renewed in 1944. The allocation of Aintree, throughout its life, was virtually all freight types with a number of shunting engines to serve the nearby sorting sidings.

*J. A. Peden*

Plate 53: With spark arresters fitted, Nos. 310, 1287 and 1289, three of the four 'Pugs' allocated to Aintree in 1921, stand at the side of the fitting shop on a Sunday afternoon. The 'Pugs' had disappeared from the allocation by 1930, never to return and Aintree's allocation had been cut from 100 locomotives at the Grouping to just under 60 by 1947.

*Lancashire & Yorkshire*
*Railway Society*

Plate 54: The North Staffordshire Railway had an engine shed at Alsager from the earliest days, but in 1900 it opened this new 'northlight' shed following LNWR practice. The view shows a typical posed set up with four immaculate 0-6-0s, Nos. 85, 94, 72 and 88, lined up for the photographer. The bowler-hatted gentleman was probably the new shed foreman, looking somewhat proud of his establishment.

*Ron Dyer Collection*

Plate 55: Alsager, on 28th May 1961. The shed had gained a new concrete roof at the beginning of the British Railways period and the allocation had altered somewhat with LMS standard types now in residence, as they had been since the 1930s. As with all depots of this size, the LMS did not see fit to spend the huge amounts of money necessary to provide mechanical servicing facilities, so Alsager was left to cope with manpower for its small coaling stage which was sited just out of picture, to the right. The depot closed on 19th June 1962.

*M. S. Houlgrave*

*Plate 56:* The Highland Railway engine shed at Aviemore was a fine example of random stone construction, with archways that were typical of that Company's shed design. This view, taken sometime during the early 1900s, has 4-4-0s No. 122 *Loch Moy* and No. 128 *Loch Luichart* with footplate and shed staff posing for the camera. The allocation of this shed never exceeded twenty locomotives, with tender engines always being in the majority, and only one or, sometimes, two tank locomotives being resident. The 55 ft. turntable was replaced by a 60 ft. vacuum unit by British Railways, but little, if any, improvements were carried out by the LMS. The depot closed in May 1962.

*A. G. Ellis*

*Plate 57:* There had been an engine shed at Ayr from 1839, but during 1877/8, the Glasgow & South Western Railway had built this six road stone-walled shed to the Company standard design. A 44 ft. turntable and timber-built coaling stage were provided. The turntable was exchanged for a 50 ft. unit at a later period but the triangle surrounding the depot, rendered anything larger unnecessary. When this view was taken, in September 1953, the ornamental openings above the engine roads had been replaced by timber cladding on the left side of the shed, the openings originally containing windows. From a peak of around seventy locomotives at the turn of the century, the allocation then settled down to the mid-fifties mark during the LMS period and stayed that way until the end of steam. In addition to a large number of freight locomotives to serve the nearby coalfields, Ayr had boasted a number of Baltic tanks from 1922 to 1935 as well as many 4-4-0 for passenger workings. The shed closed to steam in October 1966.

*Brian Hilton*

*Plate 58:* Standing on the south shore of Loch Leven, Ballachulish (Glencoe) was yet another outpost of the Caledonian Railway. The engine shed was opened in 1903 and formed, along with the goods yard and station, the typical end of the line setting so often depicted by modellers. A 60ft. turntable was installed from the shed's opening but the coaling facilities were primitive to the end with a wagon being called upon to provide a platform, as this 1951 view shows, with a fireman refuelling his 0-4-4T from the open wagon outside the shed.

*A. G. Ellis*

*Plate 59:* Ex-Caledonian Railway 0-6-0 No. 17411, fitted with a Westinghouse brake for passenger working, stands in the drizzle, in the late 1930s, outside the shed at Ballachulish. As a sub-shed of Oban, two locomotives were supplied by that shed on a weekly basis although the 0-4-4T, which made up the required pair, usually stayed for many months, whereas the 0-6-0 would change frequently.

*W. A. Camwell*

*Plate 60:* The serene setting, just after the line was opened, of Ballachulish.

*Brian Hilton Collection*

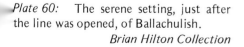

*Plate 61:* In 1923, the LMS inherited two engine sheds at the Lancashire & Yorkshire Railway establishment at Bank Hall (then known as Sandhills); an eight road dead end shed with twin hipped roofs, built in 1874/5 and known as the 'new' shed, and this building, which represented half of what was, in 1923, another eight road structure dating from 1858. The other half of the shed was demolished in 1933 to make way for the No. 2 size coaling plant, a move necessary owing to lack of space at the depot. In 1937, when this view was recorded, the old 1858 shed was used for repair purposes.

*L. W. Perkins*

*Plate 62:* Barton Wright 4-4-0 No. 10102 stands inside the 'new' shed in the late 1920s. There were 85 locomotives allocated to Bank Hall at the Grouping but by 1934, this total had dropped to just 44 engines, the same number that saw the depot into British Railways' ownership. Closure took place in October 1966.

*W. L. Good*

*Plate 63:* There had been an engine shed at Beattock from 1847 to house banking engines that pushed northbound trains up the famous bank. Sited just north of the station, the two road establishment had a 54ft. turntable and a coaling platform complete with hand crane. The number of locomotives allocated here was usually around the 15 mark, and nearly all were tank engines except for the occasional 0-6-0 being drafted in to help out. Throughout most of the LMS period four specially-built banking engines, the McIntosh/Pickersgill 0-4-4 tanks, Nos. 15237—40, were residents along with at least half a dozen other 0-4-4Ts, but during the 1940s, nine ex-Caledonian 4-6-2 tank engines supplemented the faithful four.

*C. L. Caddy*

*Plate 64:* One of the ex-Caledonian 4-6-2 tanks stands beside Beattock Shed in British Railways' days. The end of steam came to this shed on 29th April 1967.

*G. Coltas*

*Plate 65:* The Midland Railway opened this four road shed at Bedford in 1896 to replace a smaller shed opened at the time of the Midland Railway's London Extension, in 1868. The coaling plant, from where this view was taken, was erected in 1936 along with the single skip ash plant, and a 60ft. turntable had been installed at the south end of the yard a year previously. Bedford was one of only two 'northlight' sheds constructed by the Midland Railway, the other being at Bradford Manningham. This 1952 scene shows the new concrete-beamed roof in the early stages of erection. The allocation at this time consisted of about 40 locomotives and, except for the few Ivatt 2-6-2Ts, still had a strong Midland flavour. However, eleven years later, diesels had taken over the depot and steam was gone forever.

*British Rail*

*Plate 66:* Looking south towards the servicing and stabling area of Bescot Motive Power Depot, in April 1964. The smoke haze hanging over the locomotives, was usually a good guide for any first time visitor to most engine sheds, and Bescot was no exception. Opened in 1892, the depot was one of the last strongholds of LNWR steam in British Railways' days, the LMS handing over 53 ex-LNWR 0-8-0s in December 1947 out of an allocation of 75 locomotives based here. Today, the site accommodates a large diesel depot and the old steam shed, seen here on the right, is retained and houses the breakdown crane. *K. Fairey*

*Plate 67:* The unmistakable skyline of Blackpool Central Shed, on a sunny morning in April 1950. This shed started life as a short four road 'northlight' style building in 1885 but, by the end of the 1890s, it had doubled in length and had a further four roads added to the west side to accommodate the large number of locomotives serving this dormitory and holiday town. Typical of 'northlight' roofs, the shed was without proper cover for many years and it was 1957 before a start was made on a new lightweight steel and corrugated sheet roof. The planned coal and ash plants were never erected and the standard L&YR coal stage sufficed, with the aid of a mobile conveyor. Ash was removed using the age old method of shovel and sweat. The allocation, from 1900 onwards, was always around the forty plus mark, but at certain holiday periods over a hundred engines would have to be accommodated and provision was made for extra stabling roads about a quarter of a mile south, on the east side of the vast carriage sidings. The sub-shed at Blackpool North (Talbot Road), although only a three road 'northlight' affair, was subject to the same massive influx of locomotives during the summer months and was, without doubt, the busiest sub-shed on the LMS. Both sheds closed at the beginning of November 1964 and all trace of Central has now gone, the site now being used as a huge parking area for buses and cars, catering for a new generation of holidaymaker. *Brian Hilton*

*Plate 68:* Bolton Burnden, in 1938, as seen from the coaler. The older hipped roof section of the shed contrasts with the 1889 vintage 'northlight' roof on the right. It was 1875 when the L&YR established the depot here to replace a shed at Burnden Junction. The concrete-framed ash plant, erected in 1935 along with the coaler, is visible in the foreground. The whole shed was re-roofed in the late LMS period and other improvements included the installation of a 60ft. vacuum-tractored turntable, in 1940, to replace the L&YR-derived 50ft. electric unit. This depot was one of the last bastions of steam and it closed in July 1968.

*A. G. Ellis*

*Plate 69:* A pre-modernization scene at Bolton Burnden, in 1934, with ash and clinker littering the shed yard. At this time the allocation of 54 locomotives was mainly of L&YR design except for two LMS 4F 0-6-0s. Dwarfing the Aspinall 2-4-2T No. 10751, are two of the depot's four Hughes 4-6-4 tank versions of the 'Dreadnoughts', Nos. 11119 and 11117.

*W. A. Camwell*

*Plate 70:* There was an engine shed at Bromsgrove sited on the opposite side of the main line to the stabling point. The stabling point, complete with coaling stage, was the more interesting of the two locations as most, if not all, the banking engines, used to push northbound trains up the Lickey Incline, would wait here between turns. In this September 1937 view, four ex-Midland locomotives, 'Jinties' No. 7234, 7239 and 7236, in addition to the famous 0-10-0 No. 2290, nicknamed *Big Bertha*, simmer in the sunshine before the next train requires assistance.

*W. L. Good*

*Plate 71:* In this view of Bromsgrove stabling point, *Big Bertha* passes the ex-LNER Beyer-Garratt locomotive No. 69999 which is being tried out as a Lickey banker on its first visit in 1949. The Beyer-Garratt left in November 1950 but returned for another stint in 1955, this time having been converted to an oil burner, but after a few months, it was whisked back to Gorton and eventually withdrawn. Steam ceased to be used on the Lickey Incline from September 1964 and the shed, that kept the locomotives serviced, closed and, although the roof has collapsed in places, it still stands today, surrounded by weeds.

*Brian Hilton Collection*

*Plate 72:* The Highland Railway had a habit of building two road engine sheds where one road would normally suffice and Burghead was no exception. Situated about two thirds of the way up the Hopeman branch, this stone-built shed, opened in 1895, had replaced an earlier probably wooden shed dating from around 1862. This 1935 view shows the location two years before closure and 0-6-0T No. 16145 (later renumbered 7332) was branch engine for the week, being supplied by Forres Depot. This 'Jinty' was at Polmadie twelve years later making this class a rarity north of Perth, with only one example, being No. 7541, allocated to Inverness in December 1947.

*W. A. Camwell*

*Plate 73:* The six road LNWR 'northlight' shed at Buxton, in September 1960, retains its original outline. Opened in 1892, it was a sub-shed of Longsight, maintaining a stud of about 30 locomotives. When the ex-MR engine shed at Buxton closed in 1935, most of its engines and men were transferred to the ex-LNWR establishment, boosting its allocation up to about fifty locomotives. With the extra engines came modernization with a rearranged yard layout, mechanical coaling and ash disposal plants, and the depot was coded 9D. Freight was the mainstay of work for the depot's allocation but a sizeable passenger tank stud was kept for the Manchester and Ashbourne services. Recoded 9L, in 1963, Buxton maintained steam until the last year of that form of traction on British Railways, closing in March 1968.

*W. T. Stubbs*

*Plate 74:* One of the ex-NLR 0-6-0 tank engines that was used on the Cromford & High Peak Railway, from the early 1930s, waits at Buxton for examination in 1934. Classified 2F by the LMS, these 0-6-0T engines were found to be extremely useful on the steep gradients of the line having 45 tons of adhesion. Buxton was responsible for locomotives working the whole of the C&HPR until 1935, when Rowsley took over responsibility for the eastern section of the line.

*G. Coltas*

*Plate 75:* A down express passes the grandiose facade of Chalk Farm (Camden) Engine Shed, just before the turn of the century. The London & North Western Railway had two engine sheds at Chalk Farm, dating from 1848. This view shows the passenger engine shed and on the other side of the main line was a roundhouse for the goods engines. The roundhouse closed, for railway use, in 1871 but the straight shed passed to the LMS and later into British Railways' ownership and was used solely by locomotives working long distance passenger trains out of the Euston terminus.

*Author's Collection*

*Plate 76:* Ex-LNWR 'Precursor' 4-4-0 No. 5273 *Jason*, resplendent in its new LMS livery, backs into the shed at Camden, coaled up ready for its next working, on 3rd May 1924.

*W. L. Good*

*Plate 77:* In 1919, a coaling plant of the bucket conveyor type was constructed at the north end of the yard at Camden. Further improvements to the shed were carried out by the LMS with a new roof replacing the original pitched roof in 1932. A twin 150 ton bunker coaling plant and ash plant was erected and brought into use in 1936 along with yard layout improvements and a 70ft. turntable. Because of the cramped site, extensions to the shed were impossible, but the allocation of around 50 of the largest LMS passenger locomotives was coped with by the five stabling roads available. The shed closed officially to steam in September 1961 but, for a number of years afterwards, steam could still be seen rubbing shoulders with diesels. Electrification of the main line brought on closure in January 1966.

*British Rail*

*Plate 78:* The northern end of Carnforth's Furness Railway shed, c1910, with a makeshift coaling stage erected at one of the stacks. This six road shed was a neighbour of both the LNWR and MR sheds at this junction, and was the first of the three to close after 1923 when all three sheds came under the charge of the former LNWR foreman. After demolition in 1940, a start was made on a new depot that would concentrate all the LMS motive power interests under one roof, but the intervention of the war slowed this process down, and it was 1944 before the new depot, complete with mechanical servicing aids, was brought into use. The LNWR shed was demolished but the former MR roundhouse still stands to this day and is used by a private concern.

*A. G. Ellis*

*Plate 79:*    Standing on the north side of the station, and modernized by the LMS in 1934/5, Carstairs Motive Power Depot consisted of a rebuilt four road shed, a 75 ton capacity No. 2 size coaling plant, a single skip ash disposal plant, a remodelled yard layout and a single road repair shop complete with a 7 ton wheel drop. The original shed dated back to the 1850s and, at the Grouping, had a coaling stage and a 50 ft. turntable on site. The 50 ft. turntable was kept in situ after 1935 and any locomotives not able to fit on the table used the adjacent triangle for turning. In 1943, the depot gained a 20 ton capacity steam breakdown crane from Perth, No. RS1053, an ex-Caledonian unit supplied by Cravens in 1907.

*K. Fairey*

*Plate 80:* Ex-Caledonian Railway 'Pickersgill' 4-4-0 No. 14499, wearing its new 27D shed plate, stands outside the nearly completed shed at Carstairs in 1935. The positioning of shed plates just below the smokebox numberplate was a Northern Division peculiarity in the first years of the universal code. Carstairs was a 'garage' of 27A, Polmadie, until 1941 when it became 28C, under Motherwell. British Railways' codes were 64D in 1949 and 66E in 1960. The depot closed to steam in February 1967.

*W. L. Good*

*Plate 81:* The rugged mountain scenery of the Lake District makes an imposing backdrop for the ex-Furness Railway terminus at Coniston, in April 1960. The tiny shed was built at the same time as the station and originally had a steeper slated pitched roof, but this was rebuilt, around 1946, with this corrugated asbestos cover. The 42 ft. turntable was sufficient for the usual tank engine that worked the branch which, in the later LMS period, would be a Webb 1P, 2-4-2T. The shed closed in January 1958.

*A. G. Ellis*

*Plate 82:* Corkerhill was the largest of the Glasgow & South Western Railway engine sheds. Sited in southwest Glasgow, and opened in 1896, this six road shed was a through type with a 'northlight' roof and a one road repair shop with a hoist outside. A coaling stage, complete with water tank on top, was provided as was a 60 ft. turntable. At the Grouping there were just over seventy locomotives allocated here and, with the comprehensive repair facilities, made Corkerhill the Company's most important depot.

*A. G. Elli*

*Plate 83:* The LMS invested heavily at 27J, a Corkerhill was coded in 1935, erecting a No. 1 size coaling plant with two 150 ton bunkers, a double skip ash plant and also rebuilding the shed roof over the stabling roads. An extension to the repair facilit was erected during British Railways' days, the she having 96 locomotives allocated when the new owners took charge. This October 1962 view shows full yard, with a visiting 'Duchess' on the repair sho road. Recoded 30A in 1941, British Railway changed the code, yet again, in January 1949, t 67A.

*W. T. Stubt*

Plate 84: The four road ex-LNWR engine shed at Coventry was sited in the fork of the Rugby and Warwick lines. Built in 1866, as a two road dead end structure, it was enlarged in 1897 to four roads and had twin pitched roofs. The allocation never exceeded more than twenty locomotives and, by 1947, only eight 0-8-0s and six ex-MR 0-6-0s were on the books. In 1957/8, the shed roof was rebuilt and, only six months after completion, the depot closed on 17th November 1958. This 1962 view shows the shed in its new role as an engine store, with 'Jubilee' 4-6-0 locomotives, minus nameplates, making up the bulk of the residents.

*A. George*

Plate 85: No book about LMS engine sheds would be complete without a mention of Crewe North. This former LNWR depot was a conglomerate of buildings, all dating from the last century, and at one time it had 48 roads under cover. In 1896, the shed nearest the station was demolished to make way for the goods avoiding lines and so Crewe North settled down, for the next fifty years, with 36 roads under cover to house what were the premier LMS passenger locomotives. In December 1947, the 125 allocated locomotives included 20 'Princess Royal' and 'Coronation' Pacifics, 14 'Royal Scots', 22 'Jubilees', 14 'Patriots', 38 'Black 5s' and 17 other assorted engines. This 1946 view is pure history as all trace of the depot is now gone.

*Ron Dyer Collection*

Plate 86: 'Princess Royal' class 4-6-2 No. 6200, brand new, with nameplate masked, still awaiting the final coats of paint, wears a Western Division 'A' shed plate code 15 (Crewe North) inside that shed in July 1933. Coded 5A by the LMS in 1935, Crewe North kept that code until closure in May 1965.

G. Coltas

Plate 87: On 17th July 1932, an ex-North Staffordshire Railway G class 4-4-0 poses in the midday sun at Crewe North Shed. Locomotives from the 'Knotty' were daily visitors to Crewe North when the North Staffordshire engine shed, situated opposite Crewe South, closed just after the Grouping. No. 5413 (former NSR No. 598) was cut up at Crewe Works during the following year.

W. L. Good

Plate 88: On the same day that the ex-NSR 4-4-0 was on shed, 'Royal Scot' No. 6134 *Atlas*, later renamed *The Cheshire Regiment*, simmered next to the ash plant whilst waiting to move under the coaler to refill its tender.

W. L. Good

*Plate 89:* The north end of Crewe South Shed, about thirteen years after opening, and pure North Western. Coded 15S in the LNWR list, it was a sub-shed of Crewe North. At the end of the LMS period there were 175 locomotives allocated to this depot. Of these there was one ex-L&YR example, four ex-MR engines, twenty five ex-LNWR locomotives, mainly 0-8-0s, and the rest were LMS standard types plus twelve diesel shunters.

*A. G. Ellis*

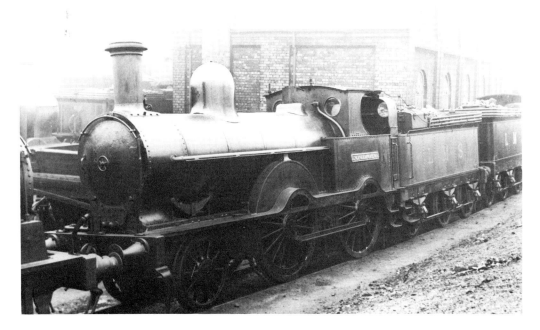

*Plate 90: Engineer Crewe*, a Waterloo class 2-4-0 formerly LNWR No. 209 *Petrel*, was maintained by Crewe South and is seen, in November 1931, stabled on the line that ran beside the east side of the shed near the offices.

*W. L. Good*

*Plate 91:* Ex-works 4-6-2 Pacific locomotive, No. 46232 *Duchess of Montrose*, sporting its new blue livery, is photographed on the 70ft. Crewe South turntable on 22nd May 1948. This turntable was installed in 1945 and enabled the depot to handle ex-works Pacifics on running-in turns.

*V. Forster*

*Plate 92:* As late as March 1966, a full house could be found at Crewe South at weekends. This depot was coded 5B from 1935 onwards and had altered, somewhat, in its appearance since it was opened, with the mechanical coaling plant appearing in 1920 and a double skip ash disposal plant being added soon after. The 'northlight' roof, or what was left of it, was replaced during 1958/9 but the new roof only covered eight of the original twelve roads. The depot closed completely in November 1967.

*W. T. Stubbs*

*Plate 93:* The ex-Glasgow & South Western Railway engine shed at Dalmellington was opened in 1856 and was one of the casualties of the 1935 economy drive, closing in that year. It was classed as a sub-shed of Ayr and stood at the end of the branch line from Holehouse. Two locomotives were usually stabled here with adequate room. In addition to the stone-built shed, a small coaling platform and a 44ft. turntable were also provided.

*W. A. Camwell*

*Plate 94:* Dawsholm was one of the few examples of 'northlight' type engine sheds in Scotland. Opened, in 1896, by the Caledonian Railway, the six road shed was also equipped with a two road fitting shop complete with a 40 ton capacity hoist. A single road coaling stage and a 50ft. turntable were also provided. The roof of the engine shed was rebuilt during 1949/50 in the ferro-concrete style. Dawsholm's allocation, throughout the LMS period, was mainly of Caledonian Railway origin and even by the end of 1946, only eight Stanier 2-6-2 tanks and two Stanier 2-8-0s had infiltrated this ex-Caledonian stronghold with an allocation of 58 engines. Shed codes were 27K in 1935, 31E in 1941 and 65D in 1949. The depot closed in October 1964.

*W. E. Boyd*

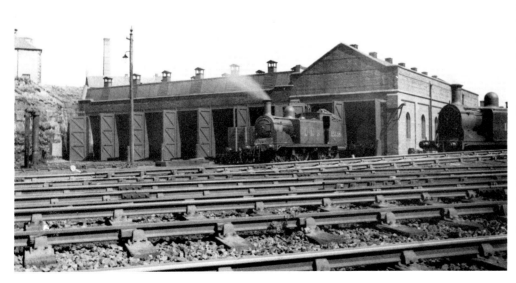

*Plate 95:* Currock, the Maryport & Carlisle Railway Depot, was sited to the south-west of Carlisle and was built around 1878. This view depicts the shed shortly after the facilities were completed. To the left can be seen the coalman's hut and the hand-operated coaling crane. The stone-built shed was last used for locomotive purposes in 1923. *D. F. Tee Collection*

*Plate 96:* Two of the Maryport & Carlisle Railway's sturdy looking four coupled locomotives stand at Currock in the early part of the twentieth century. Both these engines were later absorbed by the LMS. No. 8, a 2-4-0, was allocated the number 10006 but never carried it as this engine was cut up in 1925. The 0-4-2 locomotive, No. 4, became No. 10010. Worthy of note is the blackened stonework of the shed when compared with the previous photograph. *Real Photographs*

*Plate 97:*    Situated in the fork of the Glasgow and Leith lines, Dalry Road was the Edinburgh engine shed of the Caledonian Railway. A standard four road, dead end, brick-built building with transverse roof pitches, was provided for stabling, but a two road fitting shop with a 30 ton hoist, situated on the south side of the yard, was of timber construction. A timber-built coaling stage was on site but the turntable, a 51 ft. unit in 1900, was situated some distance away at Princes Street Station. The LMS replaced the turntable, in the 1930s, with a 60 ft. vacuum-operated unit. The photograph shows the stabling shed just two weeks before the depot closed on 3rd October 1965.

*W. T. Stubbs*

*Plate 98:*    Two ex-Caledonian Railway 0-4-4 tank engines queue for fuel beside the rickety-looking coaling stage at Dalry Road in July 1947. This stage served the depot until closure and was a typical Caledonian structure, enclosed for weather protection.

*V. Forster Collection*

*Plate 99:* A visitor to Derby Motive Power Depot would always find a number of repainted ex-works locomotives on shed, in steam, waiting to be worked back to their home depots. This shiny black Stanier 2-8-0, of Toton Depot, photographed in May 1952, would not be in this external condition again until its next visit to the works some years later.

*V. Forster Collection*

*Plate 100:* Stanier 2-6-4T No. 42636 looks the worse for wear after a trip into the turntable pit, outside Derby Shed, in May 1963. The steam breakdown crane has just sorted matters out but the battered locomotive was withdrawn just after the incident and was eventually cut up. The 70 ft. turntable did not fair any better as it was taken out and the pit was filled in. Twenty years previously, both would have been repaired, but this was the age of the diesel.

*G. Coltas*

*Plate 101 (top left):* Standing at the junction where the Highland line diverges to the Kyle of Lochalsh in the west and to Wick in the north, the engine shed at Dingwall was established about 1870. There was a 43 ft. turntable on the site but this was taken out of use before 1942. A coaling bank was built near to the station but, as this 1961 photograph shows, in later years coaling was carried out direct from wagons, with a trestle, and the wagon door acting as a stage. Twelve months after this scene was captured, the shed was closed and the ex-Caledonian 4-4-0 locomotive, seen here, was withdrawn.

*W. T. Stubbs*

*Plate 102 (bottom left):* Although not strictly LMS, the ex-Great Northern Railway engine shed at Doncaster had housed L&YR locomotives from the mid-19th century. These were used on passenger workings to that town from L&YR territory and this arrangement continued into the LMS period, with the engine being supplied by Wakefield (25A) Motive Power Depot. In this June 1939 view, Aspinall 2-4-2T No. 10855 rests outside the shed next to an ex-GCR Class 04, 2-8-0 locomotive.

*W. L. Good*

*Plate 103 (below):* Durranhill was the Midland Railway's engine shed at Carlisle. Opened in 1875, the shed was a standard 'square' roundhouse with three roof pitches. Around 1922/3, two through roads were laid down in the shed, making it unique with Toton in having this arrangement. Although it was closed from the early 1930s, the shed was to see use for locomotive purposes from 1943 onwards until it was demolished in the 1960s. This 1934 view, of the inside of the shed, shows off the MR shed design and also the shortness of the radiating roads nearest to the through roads, being of only one 0-6-0T engine length.

*W. L. Good*

*Plates 104 & 105:*    Who cleaned the windows of Dumfries engine shed before the Grouping? Certainly no one did afterwards, as these two views, taken either side of 1923, prove. The six road shed was built in the 1870s and replaced a smaller shed dating from 1848. The new shed was typical G & SW and followed closely the sheds at Ayr, Hurlford and Muirkirk, in design. Sited on the east side of the main line, Dumfries also possessed a one road fitting shop, and separated by a road bridge from the rest of the depot was a 60ft. turntable and a manual coaling stage. The allocation at the Grouping was about 40 locomotives but, being small in numbers, the ex-G & SW types were soon withdrawn under the LMS standardization policy and were replaced by LMS standards and ex-Caledonian engines by 1933. In December 1947, LMS Compounds, in addition to 2P 4-4-0s, carried out all of the passenger work, with 'Crabs' and ex-Caledonian 0-6-0s making up the allocation of 40 locomotives, with the LNWR represented by 2-4-2 tanks, Nos. 6635 and 6639.

*A. G. Ellis and Real Photographs*

*Plate 106:* On 30th April 1966, when this scene was captured, Dumfries had only two days left before closure. The shed had lost its ornate windows by 1947 and the allocation had been whittled down to less than twenty locomotives by 1965. On the right is the office block and repair shop with the engine hoist just visible. LMS shed code 12G was bestowed on the depot in 1935 and British Railways gave it the code 68B in January 1949. The final code, 67E, was applied from July 1962.

*D. F. Tee*

*Plate 107:* Edge Hill was the largest LMS shed in the Liverpool area and could boast twenty stabling roads under cover at the western end of the shed. There had been a shed here from the earliest days of railways, but the LNWR had built up the site with the addition of sheds during the latter half of the 19th century. Finally, in 1902, the last shed was erected, this being of a 'northlight' design backing on to the massive twenty road hipped roof shed. From the turn of the century there were over 140 locomotives allocated to Edge Hill. This 1949 view shows the usual crop of passenger, goods and shunting engines to be found here in the late LMS and early British Railways periods. Demolition followed soon after closure, in May 1968.

*Real Photographs*

*Plate 108:* Ex-LNWR 0-8-4T No. 7935 gets ready to move off from the Edge Hill coaler. These massive tank engines were used for shunting the adjacent Gridiron Yard.

*Real Photographs*

*Plate 109:* The ex-LNWR engine shed at Farnley Junction played host to these immaculate 'Singles' in June 1925 whilst they were en route to the Darlington Centenary Celebrations. The Midland Railway 'Spinner', No. 679, was cut up in 1928 but the LNWR 2-2-2 *Cornwall* was preserved.

*T. Shuttleworth*

*Plate 110:* A company house at Farnley Junction Engine Shed was provided for the shedmaster. These houses were to be found at most of the larger engine sheds and were usually sited very near to the shed itself. To the left is the lodging house, or barracks as they were also known, where 42 beds were provided for visiting footplatemen. This May 1966 scene shows the neglected state of the grounds, which all too often was the case in British Railways' days. The depot at Farnley Junction closed in November 1966.

*D. Rowland*

*Plate 111:* The lattice main roof girders of Gloucester engine shed gives away the fact that this shed was a standard 'square' roundhouse of Midland Railway origin, combining the features of the second style of this type of shed with three straight front to back roof pitches. The shed was opened in 1895 and replaced a roundhouse shed nearby. In addition to the usual coaling stage, a four road fitting shop was also provided. Ex-Midland 0-4-0T No. 41530, seen here in April 1955, was a regular performer on the local docks branch along with two or three other members of the class.

H. C. Casserley

*Plate 112:* At the Grouping, there were three of these elegant Johnson 'Singles' allocated to Gloucester and No. 678, seen at the rear of the shed in June 1923, looks brand new but, with over thirty years service behind her, she had only a couple of years left before being cut up for scrap at Derby. The 0-6-0 freight locomotives made up the majority of this depot's allocation during its lifetime together with just a few passenger types. After closure, in May 1964, the shed was demolished and the site was cleared.

A. G. Ellis

*Plate 113:* When Greenock Ladyburn was opened by the Caledonian Railway in 1884, it had ten through roads spanned by a 'westernlight' roof. The coaling stage was of timber construction and a 52ft. turntable, together with a one road fitting shop, adjacent to the shed, completed the facilities. This post-World War II view shows what remained of the shed when British Railways took ownership. There were 40 locomotives allocated in December 1947 including eleven Fowler 2-6-4 side window tanks and a solitary ex-Caledonian 4-6-2T No. 15355.

Photomatic

Plate 114: When it was rebuilt in the 1950s, only five of the stabling roads at Ladyburn were covered by the new single-pitched roof; obviously sufficient for the dwindling allocation. In this June 1965 view, eight of the depot's twelve remaining steam locomotives are seen on shed.

K. Fairey

Plate 115: Opened in 1869, by the Glasgow & South Western Railway, Greenock Princes Pier had, by 1923, an allocation of thirty locomotives. This 1935 view depicts the shed building in its original condition except for the addition of the extra high smoke stacks erected in the 1890s after complaints from local tenants and, probably, the shed staff. A 50 ft. turntable was supplied from the outset and was situated behind the water tank seen on the right. The coaling shelter was provided by the LMS, a previous structure having given up the ghost, but coal still had to be thrown manually from wagon to tender.

Ron Dyer Collection

Plate 116: Greenock Princes Pier in September 1953. The arches had been replaced by a steel girder in the 1940s and the smoke vents had been altered, but little change had, otherwise, taken place. The allocation dropped to about ten locomotives and this shed was now a sub-shed of Ladyburn. Fowler 4-4-0 locomotives were the mainstay of the motive power at this depot together with a few tank engines. The shed closed in May 1959.

Brian Hilton

*Plate 117:* Beyer-Garratt, No. 4969 stands on the entrance/exit road to Hasland roundhouse in 1936. Hasland Shed was opened in 1875 by the Midland Railway to serve the nearby coalfields. Ten Beyer-Garratts were allocated to this depot on the last day of LMS owner-ship, a class of locomotive which had first worked from Hasland Depot in 1933. No special accommodation was ever erected for these giants and they were always stabled in the yard. No. 4969 was renumbered, along with the rest of the class, in 1938 and became No. 7969. It was withdrawn by British Railways in August 1957 and was cut up during the same month at Crewe Works.

*R. J. Essery Collection*

*Plate 118:* Hasland Shed yard, in August 1947, with four of the depot's five ex-LTSR 4-4-2Ts in store. Left to right are Nos. 2109, 2092, 2102 and 2095. Behind the stored locomotives can be seen the depot's 15 ton capacity steam breakdown crane No. RS1030/15 which came to Hasland from Sheffield Grimesthorpe in 1931. This crane was ex-MR No. 248, purchased by them from Cowans Sheldon in 1901. The coaling stage had long since been demo-lished and was replaced by a Stranraer type coaling plant which was erected in 1935. Coded 18C in the 1935 list, Hasland was recoded 16H in September 1963. The depot closed one year later and what remained of the roofless shed was demolished soon after.

*C. A. Appleton*

*Plate 119:* Hellifield ex-Lancashire & Yorkshire Railway engine shed was one of the casualties of the Grouping, being closed down on 2nd November 1927 when its locomotives and men were transferred to the ex-Midland Railway establishment sited at the northern end of the station. The three road shed was opened in 1881 and was the last hipped roof engine shed built by the L&YR. An unusual feature of the building was the water tank sitting on top of the whole length of the office/stores/mess accommodation. A water tank was also provided on top of the single road coaling stage and a 50ft. manual turntable completed the facilities. When the L&YR merged with the LNWR, five locomotives were allocated to Hellifield. These were Class 5, 2-4-2T engines Nos. 516 and 1009; Class 6, 2-4-2T No. 480; Class 27, 0-6-0 No. 1060 and Class 31, 0-8-0 No. 1641. On closure, the foreman took charge of the former Midland shed.

*J. Fishwick*

*Plate 120:* Ex-ROD 2-8-0 No. 9471, (formerly No. 9640), of shed 37 Mold Junction, stands in the afternoon sun at Holyhead Shed in the summer of 1931. Although the shed serviced mainly express passenger locomotives, freight engines were not unusual at this ex-LNWR establishment. Coded shed 22 in the LNWR list and in the later LMS Western Division 'A' list, Holyhead became 7C in 1935 and 6J in May 1952.

*R. J. Essery Collection*

*Plate 121:* Holyhead Shed at the end of the LMS era with the usual line up of express passenger locomotives. The shed roof was about to be replaced after 88 years service; more time than the combined ages of this line-up. In addition to the resident and visiting 4-6-0s, LMS, and later BR, Pacifics made regular appearances on the boat/mail trains and, in 1955, five new 'Britannias' were eventually allocated to Holyhead. A 70ft. manual turntable was laid down at the south end of the yard in 1926 and, by 1936, a small Lynn type mechanical coaling plant was in use. Although only sixteen locomotives were allocated, on 31st December 1947, the list included four 'Royal Scots', five 'Black 5s', three LMS Compounds and four tank engines. The depot closed to steam in December 1966.

*Author's Collection*

*Plate 122:* The tiny two road 'northlight' engine shed at Horwich was situated in the Works complex and was tucked away between No. 1 erecting shop, on the right, and the paint shop, also with a 'northlight' roof. Opened in 1887, it replaced a small shed at Horwich Station and, in December 1921, the following locomotives were allocated: L&YR Chief Mechanical Engineer's 'Coupe', No. 731; Class 21 0-4-0ST, No. 226, Class 27 0-6-0 locomotives Nos. 106, 210, 341, 882, 1032 and 1147 and Class 28 0-6-0 No. 625. The shed was coded 15 in the L&YR list but, in July 1928, closed as a 'running shed' and from that day on, was home for the standard gauge Works shunters. This scene is a real piece of social history and was captured around 1910. *National Railway Museum*

*Plate 123:* A pre-grouping view of the east end of Huddersfield Hillhouse Shed yard with Class G1 0-8-0, No. 1298 (later LMS No. 9361) framed by the office block, and Class G2 0-8-0, No. 134 (LMS No. 9425) about to 'book off' shed. The LNWR had established an engine shed here as early as 1850 and, during the following sixty years, they had rebuilt and enlarged the shed on a number of occasions. By 1934, the allocation of 52 locomotives had only 24 ex-LNWR types amongst the ranks and further changes at Hillhouse, brought about by the LMS, included the installation of mechanical coal and ash plants in 1936 and a new roof in 1938. The shed closed in January 1967 and the site was cleared. The vast empty space, where it once stood, next to the adjacent Hillhouse sidings, is still vacant to this day.

*D. J. Clarke Collection*

*Plate 124:* Huddersfield, circa 1924, with 'Prince of Wales' class 4-6-0, No. 331 (later LMS No. 5802) heading a line of locomotives projecting out of what was once a wagon repair shop, taken over during rebuilding in 1906. The 4-6-0s were used mainly for the fast freight traffic to London and were allocated to Hillhouse well into the 1930s. The older Webb 1P 2-4-2T, No. 2141, behind, outlived these larger engines and became BR No. 46680. The year 1947 saw only two ex-LNWR locomotives allocated to 25B, as the depot was then coded. Both were Class G1 0-8-0s. The stud of 42 engines included Fowler 2-6-4Ts, 'Crabs', Stanier 8Fs and 'Black 5s' and five ex-L & YR engines.

*British Rail*

*Plate 125:* The Leek & Manifold Valley Light Railway was inherited by the LMS in 1923 and just eleven years later, the 2ft. 6in. gauge line was closed. Opened in 1904, the line owned only two locomotives, both 2-6-4Ts, that were kept in this two road shed at Hulme End at the northern extremity of the railway. In July 1959, the shed had found employment as a lock-up garage for motor vehicles and the adjacent terminus building on the left was used as a store.

*W. T. Stubbs*

*Plate 126:* Sited within the junction between the Kilmarnock–Dumfries–Galston lines, Hurlford Motive Power Depot stood at what was the centre of the Glasgow & South Western Railway empire and, in 1914, had an allocation of one hundred locomotives. Opened in 1877, to replace the cramped premises near Kilmarnock Station, the shed was of period design and the yard facilities included a single road coaling stage and a 45ft. turntable. The turntable was replaced, in 1919, by a 60ft. unit and, prior to this date, a 35 ton capacity engine hoist had been erected on the shed in the yard at the rear. On closure of the depot, some forty seven years later, these same facilities survived, together with additional pits put in by the LMS, as the only form of modernization carried out during that time. This July 1960 view, taken from the coaling stage, shows a strangely empty yard in front of the original stone-built shed. Throughout most of the LMS and British Railways period, the depot was home for about fifty locomotives, mainly of the 4-4-0 and 0-6-0 wheel arrangement classes.

*W. T. Stubbs*

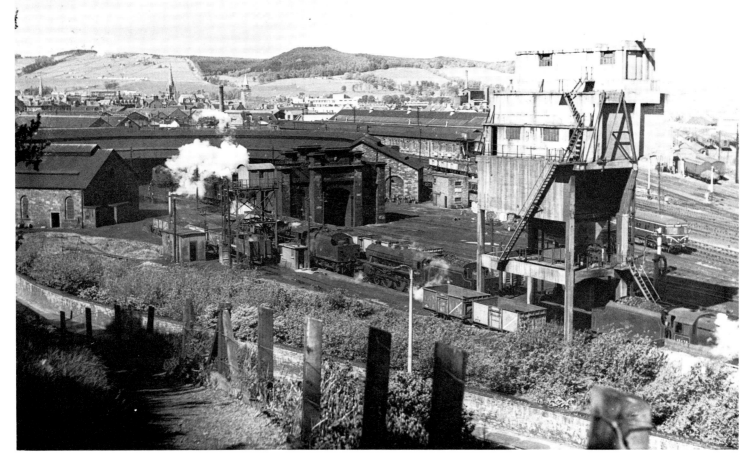

*Plate 127:*   An overall view of the ex-Highland Railway roundhouse at Inverness, in May 1960. The shed was opened for use in 1863 although, at first, only 21 of the eventual 31 roads were covered. The other ten were covered by the turn of the century. Locomotives gained entry to the shed through the magnificent stone portal which was actually a disguised 45,000 gallon water tank. At a later date, entrance/exit roads were laid at both sides of the archway. Mechanical coal and ash plants were erected in 1935 when much of the ex-Highland Railway locomotive stud was still in residence. With the coming of diesels to the Highland Region, the shed closed in May 1962 and was eventually demolished, including the archway.

*A. R. Goult*

*Plate 128:*   A pre-grouping view of the Inverness roundhouse with No. 140 *Taymouth Castle* standing on the turntable. From the building of this depot the turntable pit was boarded over, but the LMS opened up the pit when the shed was altered, in the 1930s, by taking away the arched doorways of each numbered stabling road.

*Real Photographs*

*Plate 129:* Drummond 0-6-4T No. 15300 (ex-HR No. 39) is being prepared by its fireman on one of the open roads at Inverness in 1933.

*B. Matthews Collection*

*Plate 130:* Inverness roundhouse, in September 1952, with the depot's 63 ft. 4 in. turntable about to be moved, to allow one of the shed's numerous 'Black 5s' to leave for work.

*D. F. Tee*

*Plate 131:* A wide angle view of Inverness roundhouse, in August 1955.

*P. Tatlow*

*Plate 132:* The former Midland shed at Kettering was opened in 1876 to replace a smaller shed which had been built ten years previously. The four road shed was typical of Midland architecture for the period, with ornamental brickwork and arched openings. In this July 1948 view, one of the depot's three Compounds, No. 1010, still sports its LMS number whilst renumbered 3F, No. 43629, is awaiting its BR tender logo. Seven months earlier, the allocation consisted of thirty eight locomtives, two of which were ex-LNWR 0-8-0s and one of the last ex-Midland Railway 1P 2-4-0s, No. 20216.

*H. C. Casserley*

*Plate 133:* This October 1963 scene shows the position of Kettering Depot in relation to the station. The coaling stage was one of the MR 'single' types and situated behind it were more stabling roads and, in later years, a 60ft. turntable. The shed closed in June 1965 with demolition following soon after.

*W. T. Stubbs*

Plate 134: Another idyllic end of the line setting, was at Kirkcudbright, situated at the terminus of the branch from Castle Douglas. Opened by the Glasgow & South Western Railway in 1864, this stone-built shed housed the branch engines, supplied by Dumfries, until 1955 when the tiny shed closed. A 42 ft. turntable served the location but coaling facilities were non-existent, a wagon being used when the coal was required. The drivers' and firemen's mess room was situated underneath the dwelling house built on to the south-east corner of the shed.

*W. T. Stubbs*

Plate 135: Kyle of Lochalsh, in July 1958, with the 61 year old shed still in its original condition, except for the doors that were fitted until the 1940s. The Stanier 4-6-0s were supplied by Inverness and were the mainstay of the motive power at Kyle of Lochalsh until displaced by diesels in 1962. A 60 ft. turntable was supplied and the coaling facilities consisted of a coaling bank with hand shovel power. Notice the snowplough brackets hanging from the buffer beam of No. 45479.

*P. Tatlow*

*Plate 136:* With the imprint of the pitched roof still visible on the water tank in 1959, this was all that remained of the LNWR shed at Lancaster. Opened in 1875, the shed was one of the victims of the LMS economy drives to dispose of excessive facilities in certain areas. The shed closed in February 1934 and its engines and men were transferred to the former Midland Railway establishment at Green Ayre.

*W. T. Stubbs*

*Plate 137:* Room for one more at Lancaster Green Ayre in the summer of 1963. This ex-MR shed was unusual in that the only way a locomotive could enter the shed was via the 60 ft. vacuum-operated turntable. The shed was built in the 1860s and in addition to the four roads under cover, it also had a one road repair shop sited where the lean-to structure stands on the right of the photograph. The original roof of the shed consisted of two hipped sections with raised smoke vents but this was replaced during the rebuilding of the shed in 1943. This depot had more codes than most during the LMS and British Railways' period. It started as Midland Railway shed 32; it became M32 in 1934; 11C in 1935; 20H in 1936; 23C in 1950; 11E in 1951; 24J in 1957 and 10J in 1963, closing with this code in April 1966.

*A. George*

*Plate 138:* Situated towards the western end of the Leadhills & Wanlockhead Light Railway, Leadshills was chosen as the site for this small timber engine shed, as the line from Elvanfoot was not extended beyond Leadhills until the following year. Opened in 1901, the shed was home for various Caledonian 0-4-4Ts over the years, until the mid-1930s when an LMS 'Sentinel' steam rail motor was used on the 6¾ mile branch. The line closed in December 1938 and the exposed position of the location, around the tiny shed, can be appreciated from this 1935 photograph. Also to be seen is evidence of past mining activity in the lead-bearing hills.

*W. A. Camwell*

*Plate 139:* When the North Midland Railway opened its terminus at Leeds, Hunslet Lane, in 1840, this eight road engine shed was provided along with a 42ft. turntable and a coking shed, that stood just beyond the visible ash pit. The shed was vacated in 1868 when the Midland Railway concentrated all its motive power at the new Holbeck establishment. The facilities at Hunslet Lane were used as a goods depot from then on and were still used as such well into British Railways' days as can be seen in this August 1967 view.

*D. F. Tee*

*Plate 140:* Lees, standing on what was then the Lancashire/Yorkshire border. This ex-LNWR depot was opened in 1878 to replace a one road shed at Oldham Mumps. A period 'northlight' roof spanned six roads and the usual facilities were provided. In the 1930s, ex-L&YR locomotives began to outnumber the LNWR designs and, with the gradual influx of LMS standard types, the changeover was complete by 1947. This April 1955 view shows the shed just before the roof was taken down to make way for the new cover which was finished by the end of 1956.

*A. C. Gilbert*

*Plate 141:* March 1960, and the WD 2-8-0s had arrived in strength at Lees, there being nine of them out of a total of fifteen locomotives allocated. War Department locomotive No. 90402 stands on what was No. 1 road but this was cut short during the rebuilding of the shed, four years previously, making Lees a five road shed. After the shed was closed in April 1964, the site was cleared and a housing estate now hides any trace of the depot.

*K. Fairey*

*Plate 142:* Lees, in August 1953, with the usual summer rain falling over Oldham. Locomotives, from left to right, are Nos. 49618, 40014 and 49668. The ex-L&YR coach, No. M168826M, is a vintage six wheeler used, at this time, to carry breakdown gear. The LNWR sawtooth style of 'northlight' roof is clearly visible.

*F. W. Shuttleworth*

*Plate 143:* A scene that every 'shed basher' liked to see on a Sunday visit to any large shed. This was Leicester, in September 1962, with BR Standards taking up a fair percentage of the available stabling space. The coaling plant and two ash disposal plants were late additions to the facilities at Leicester being erected during 1954/5. The modern concrete roundhouse stood out of the picture on the right.

*H. A. Gamble*

*Plate 144:* The old 1840s' roundhouse forms the background for this May 1933 view of Leicester Motive Power Depot, with 3F 0-6-0 No. 3419, minus its middle set of wheels, and 0-6-4T No. 2005 with only three years more service in front of it before being scrapped by Derby Works.

*G. Coltas*

*Plate 145:* The new roundhouse at Leicester, in 1952. Immediately behind the Fowler 2-6-4T, wagons occupy the roads of the old straight shed, erected in 1893 and demolished to make way for yard improvements that were taking place when this 'official' was taken. The old 60 ft. turntable, in the foreground, was retained for further use.

*British Rail*

*Plate 146:* The ex-LNWR shed at Leighton Buzzard was built in 1860 to serve the branch line to Dunstable. Freight traffic gave the shed much of its work with the local quarries providing the majority of revenue. Always a sub-shed of Bletchley, the shed closed in November 1962.

*A. R. Goult*

*Plate 147:* Johnson Midland 0-6-0T No. 41686 is seen being coaled at Lincoln St. Marks in 1949. The coaling stage was rebuilt in 1931 and, at the same time, the crane was fitted with an electric motor. The shed, seen on the left, was rebuilt five years previously and, at the time, four locomotives were allocated. Coming under Eastern Region control, in May 1953, this former Midland outpost closed six years later.

*R. J. Essery Collection*

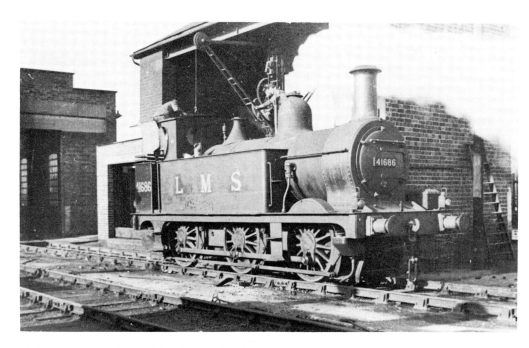

*Plate 148:* The ex-LNWR shed at Llandovery, on the Central Wales line, had one major role to carry out in addition to providing locomotives for any local work. This was to house the banking engines required for trains ascending Sugar Loaf Summit. No. 42394 would be one of the designated bankers when this photograph captured the engine outside the well preserved 55 year old 'northlight' shed in May 1957.

*A. R. Goult*

*Plate 149:* Longsight, in March 1954, and the roof is about to be pulled down to make way for a new shed. This was all that remained of the large twelve road shed inherited from the LNWR. Although mechanical coaling and ash plants were erected in 1934, the LMS did nothing about the shed building, which was really two twelve road sheds, back to back, that were joined by four through roads on the east side of the shed. The southern half of the shed had a hipped roof and dated from 1870, although Longsight had been used for locomotive purposes from 1840. The northern half of the shed was built in 1903 and was of period construction with a 'northlight' roof. This shed was replaced, during 1948/9, by an eight road concrete and brick building similar to the LMS standard shed. The hipped roof shed was replaced in 1956 by a six road shed. Both sheds are still in use today for the maintenance and stabling of diesel locomotives and multiple units.

*British Rail*

*Plates 150 & 151:*    During the latter half of World War II, the War Department loaned, to the LMS, a large number of locomotives that were due to go overseas once the allies had established railheads on the Continent. Although Longsight did not have any of these locomotives allocated, they were regular visitors, and these two views show an Austerity 2-10-0, No. 3696 and an American-built 2-8-0, No. 1907, both from Crewe South, stabled on the through roads of Longsight Depot, on the same day in September 1944.

*M. Bentley Collection*

*Plate 152:* Lostock Hall on Saturday, 3rd August 1968, the penultimate day of steam. Locomotives were being prepared for the following day's 'End of Steam' rail tours and, on the right, can be seen those that would never steam again. The diesels were in force but they did not stay for long, making way for 'on track' tamping machines that now use this former L&YR shed as a maintenance base.

*J. A. Sommerfield*

*Plate 153:* Low Moor, in 1947. Rebuilt during 1944/5, this former twelve road shed, built by the Lancashire & Yorkshire Railway in 1889, was halved in width to six roads as the allocation had dwindled to less than fifty engines from a peak, in 1922, of 123. The 'Jubilee' is a visitor, as the depot's nine 4-6-0s were all 'Black 5s'. This was one of the last Yorkshire depots to close, steam taking its final bow in October 1967.

*J. B. Hodgson*

*Plate 154:* An immaculate Aspinall Atlantic, No. 1404, just six years old when this picture was taken, poses at Low Moor in July 1905. At the Grouping, the largest concentration of this class, totalling fourteen in number, was allocated to Low Moor. No. 1404 became LMS No. 10312 and was withdrawn in 1930.

*Author's Collection*

*Plate 155:* Opened in 1882, Mansfield was a standard Midland Railway straight shed and replaced a smaller building sited nearby. During Midland days, the depot was a sub-shed of Nottingham and was coded 18A. In this 1936 view, ex-LTSR 4-4-2T, No. 2098, carries the depot's LMS code (16D) on its smokebox door. This locomotive was one of eight ex-Tilbury tanks that found work here on passenger trains in the latter half of the LMS period. On 31st December 1947 the allocation of thirty seven locomotives included three 4-4-0s, six Stanier 2-8-0s, twenty 3F and 4F 0-6-0s and eight assorted tank engines.

*H. C. Casserley*

*Plate 156:*     Stanier 2-6-2 tanks took over most of Mansfield's passenger services in British Railways' days, but they survived the depot and were transferred away, on closure, in April 1960.

*R. J. Essery Collection*

Plate 157: An interior view of Millhouses Shed, photographed around 1910. This was a typical Midland Railway straight shed and, with eight roads, was the largest on the system. The large amount of timber required for the smoke troughs is apparent as is the glazing in the roof. On the last day of the LMS, there were forty one locomotives allocated, the majority of which could be described as passenger types, with eight 'Jubilees' heading the list in addition to eleven ex-MR and LMS Compounds. The shed closed in January 1962 and survives to this day under private ownership.

*V. Forster Collection*

Plate 158: Looking east, along the Calder Valley main line at Mirfield, in the late summer of 1932. The engine shed is on the left and the Lancashire & Yorkshire standard coaling stage is rendering service to a Hughes 0-8-0 goods engine. The stone-built 'northlight' shed was opened in 1885 and it was the home of a mainly freight orientated locomotive stud for 82 years before its closure. In addition to the ex-L&YR 0-8-0, LNWR-built 0-8-0 No. 9271 and an unidentified LMS Class G3 0-8-0 are present; all three types representing the largest LMS freight engines, except for the Beyer-Garratts, until the introduction of the Stanier 2-8-0s. The stabling shed at Mirfield survives to this day in its 1935 rebuilt form, and is used by a road haulage contractor. However, the office/stores section, seen in the photograph, is derelict although it still retains the original 'northlight' roof.

*Author's Collection*

*Plate 159:* LMS 0-6-0s, Nos. 12494, 12110, 12499 and 12341 line up outside Moor Row in August 1939. The former Furness & LNW Joint shed suffered from mining subsidence in 1940 when the two left-hand roads and the shed covering them became unsafe, resulting in demolition following shortly afterwards. The remaining portion of the shed received a new front which was built of timber. In December 1947, the shed was home to fourteen locomotives, ten ex-Furness and L&YR 0-6-0s and four LMS 0-6-0 tank engines. Closure came in July 1954 with the shed having kept its 1935 code of 12E until then.

*W. Potter*

*Plate 160:* The first engine shed at Muirkirk was built in 1849 and was replaced by this Glasgow & South Western Railway standard shed in the early 1870s. A 50 ft. turntable was laid down on the south side of the building and a coaling shelter completed the facilities. Like many of the engine sheds which the LMS inherited in Scotland, they made little or no effort to modernize Muirkirk. The G&SW shedded usually about a dozen engines here and the Caledonian Railway used the facilities for two of their locomotives as Muirkirk was the meeting place for the branch from Poneil Junction. The 1933 allocation comprised 4-4-0s Nos. 14123 and 14137, 0-6-0s No. 17118, 17331 and 17484 and 0-4-4Ts Nos. 15149 and 15260. This shed enthusiasts' trip captures a quiet scene in July 1954. Ten years later the depot closed, having been a sub-shed of Hurlford since the 1930s.

*A. R. Goult*

*Plate 161:*    A busy yard scene at Newton Heath, in 1948. The two double skip ash disposal plants and the associated narrow gauge tubs are clearly visible. The 60ft. turntable, at this end of the yard, was complimented by a 70ft. unit in the rear yard. This vast depot had 232 locomotives allocated, in 1922, but by December 1947 this figure had dropped to 175 representing virtually every type of LMS motive power with the exception of Pacifics and Beyer-Garratts.

*W. D. Cooper*

*Plate 162:*    Baltic tank locomotive No. 11114 stands outside Newton Heath repair shop in 1931. There were four of this ten strong class allocated to the depot at this time, but this engine was one of Agecroft's pair and was exhibited at the Wembley Exhibition in 1925. Behind the locomotives can be seen the hydraulic accumulator tower and, beyond that, the 66 bed 'barracks'.

*G. Coltas*

*Plate 163:* All twenty single roof pitches of the stabling shed at Newton Heath are visible in this 'official' photograph. The probable reason for the taking of this view was the new installation of electric lighting above the doors.

*British Rail*

*Plate 164:* The full width of the stabling shed at Newton Heath (26A) can be gleaned from this 1950s' view. The hipped roof of the repair shop can be seen on the right.

*Brian Hilton*

*Plate 165:* The new 70 ft. vacuum-operated turntable in Newton Heath's back yard is nearly ready for use in this 1936 view. The sleeper-built structure supported the wagon road of the temporary coaling stage, erected during alterations to the front yard, which included the building of a 300 ton capacity coaling plant and ash plants on the site of one of the depot's two coaling stages.

*A. G. Ellis Collection*

*Plate 166:* When the Caledonian Railway completed the Callander & Oban line in 1880, they erected this timber-built engine shed at Oban in addition to a similar stone structure at Callander. The latter shed closed in 1929 but Oban remained in use until the end of steam on the line. A 50 ft. turntable and a small coaling stage were provided for the dozen or so locomotives that were allocated by 1900. The LMS erected a 'Stranraer' type 40 ton capacity coaling plant in the 1930s and a 60 ft. turntable was laid down in the yard. This was one of the smallest 'coded' depots on the LMS and in 1935 it was coded 29E. By 1941, the code was changed to 31C and British Railways' ownership brought further codes with 63E being introduced in January 1949, 63D in April 1955 and, finally, 63C in November 1959. The shed closed in March 1962.

*N. D. Mundy*

*Plate 167:* The rear of Oban shed, as seen when entering the town by train. The date is August 1957 and on the yard can be seen a couple of 'Black 5s', by this time, the workhorses of the line. In 1947, there were only five locomotives allocated to Oban, and all were ex-CR engines. They were 0-6-0s, Nos. 17396 and 17411 and 0-4-4Ts, Nos. 15187, 15215 and 15263. Larger locomotives working into Oban were, by this time, supplied by Perth Depot.

*A. R. Goult*

*Plate 168:* Penrith, in May 1951, as Ivatt 2-6-0 No. 46449 basks in the sunshine before the holiday season brings trippers to the Lake District and plenty of work for the Cockermouth, Keswick and Penrith branch engine. The shed was erected, in 1865, by the LNWR for both their use and that of the CK&PR. The shed was extended, in 1873, to enable the North Eastern Railway to stable locomotives. Penrith was a sub-shed of Carlisle (Upperby) for most of its existence but, in 1936, it was coded 12C after Durranhill, whose code this was, had closed. In 1958, the little two road shed reverted back to its former status as a sub-shed of Upperby and closure came in June 1962. The allocation on 31st December 1947 was pure LNWR with six 'Cauliflower' 0-6-0s, Nos. 28318, 28492, 28551, 28575, 28580 and 28589, making up what was a unique batch for a 'garage' depot.

*H. C. Casserley*

*Plate 169:* Coded 29A, in the LMS list, Perth Motive Power Depot was officially opened on 29th May 1938 and replaced the former Caledonian Railway shed on which site it stood and the ex-Highland Railway's establishment in that city. The eight road through shed had brick walls with steel framework supporting the asbestos-clad period style roof. The two road repair shop, seen as the taller building in this photograph, was equipped with two 40 ton capacity overhead cranes as well as a machine shop. A No. 1 size coaling plant, with twin 150 ton bunkers and a double skip ash disposal plant, was supplied for the opening of the new shed. The interesting assortment of vehicles in this view of the southern end of the shed in British Railways' days, includes two Western Region 0-6-0 pannier tanks which had been exiled to the North of Scotland for most of their lives. Recoded 63A by British Railways, the depot closed to steam in May 1967.

*G. B. McArthur*

*Plate 170:* Every other locomotive was a 'Black 5', or so it seemed, at Perth, but the ratio was more than that, with sixty of these Stanier 4-6-0s on the books on the eve of nationalization. This depot boasted the biggest concentration in the country of these trusted locomotives. Other engines on the last day of the LMS, numbered forty seven with pre-grouping designs accounting for over half of these.

*R. Anderson Collection*

*Plate 171:* Perth LMS Motive Power Depot, as seen from the top of the coaling plant, in the 1950s.
*Photomatic*

*Plate 172:* Ex-Caledonian Railway Pickersgill 0-6-0, No. 17663, stands outside the former Caledonian engine shed at Perth around 1933.

*W. L. Good*

*Plate 173:* A view, photographed prior to the Grouping, of the Highland Railway engine shed at Perth, with 4-4-0 No. 130 *Loch Fannich* holding the centre stage. Sited to the north of Perth General, this eight road stone-built shed was closed in May 1938 when the new LMS depot was opened. Known as Perth North, during LMS days, and coded 29A, along with the former Caledonian shed, hardly any improvements were carried out except to demolish the end gable in the 1920s losing the attractive arches; the stone being replaced by a timber-clad screen. A 55 ft. turntable and manual coaling stage completed the facilities.

*Author's Collection*

*Plate 174:* Highland motive power line-up at Perth, around 1902, with cleanliness being the order of the day. The four locomotives on the right continued to give good service to the LMS long after the Grouping, but the 2-4-0s next to them were withdrawn before 1923.

*A. G. Ellis*

*Plate 175:* The locomotive shed and yard at Plaistow in 1920, not long after its opening. This depot had replaced a smaller establishment which was sited nearby. Notice the ornate coaling stage which was able to coal locomotives on both sides but with only one wagon road, as opposed to two which was more usual. In addition to the eight numbered stabling roads, the single No. 9 road, on the right, led into the fitting shop where lifting facilities were available. At the Grouping, the LTSR lines possessed ninety four locomotives, all of which were suburban tank engines except for two 0-6-0 tender engines dating from 1899. Although managed by the Midland Railway from 1912, the LTSR was, as far as the locomotive stock was concerned, a separate railway, but LMS ownership was to change things, especially during the 1930s.

*Locomotive Publishing Co.*

*Plate 176:* In 1934, a total of thirty seven Stanier 3 cylinder 2-6-4 tank locomotives were introduced on the LTS lines and, in this late 1930s' view of Plaistow Depot, two of the class can be seen stabled on Nos. 3 and 4 roads. Coded 13A by the LMS, the depot became 33A in February 1949 when it came under Eastern Region control along with the remaining LTS depots. Ten years later, this east London depot lost its code and became a sub-shed of Tilbury, a much smaller four road depot some distance away. Closure came to Plaistow in June 1962.

*British Rail*

*Plate 177:* Plodder Lane, Bolton was yet another LNWR 'northlight' shed that survived into British Railways' days with its original roof. A sizeable portion of its allocation was still of LNWR origin, as this August 1947 view shows. Plodder Lane, which was coded 10D in 1935, was opened in 1875 to replace a small shed near to the same site. In 1890, this six road extension was built to supplement the four road shed, which was demolished in 1944 to make way for a 55ft. turntable. The depot was bypassed during the LMS modernization period with the nearby ex-L&YR shed at Burnden receiving the investment in the shape of mechanical coaling and ash plants. The December 1947 allocation comprised 0-8-0s, Nos. 9147 and 9378, 0-6-0s, Nos. 4079, 4119, 4341, 4352, 4356, 4379 and 4386, 0-6-2Ts, Nos. 7619, 7720, 7737, 7756, 7769, 7789, 7799 and 7802, and 0-6-0T No. 7401. The depot closed in October 1954.

*C. H. S. Owen*

*Plates 178 to 180:* These three photographs show the Caledonian Railway engine shed at Polmadie, just after the turn of the century. The massive timber shed was built, in the early 1880s, to house the growing locomotive stud of the Caledonian Railway, on the south side of the River Clyde. Fourteen roads, under cover, were used for stabling purposes and, on the east side of the building, there was a two road repair shop.

*National Railway Museum*

*Plate 181:* A panoramic view of Polmadie in May 1930. This 'official' photograph was taken to show the completed work that had taken place during the 1920s, to renew the shed and repair shop. Seven of the shed's fourteen roads continued through the buildings, with others terminating inside. The well-equipped two road repair shop, with the 'Claughton' class locomotive seen outside, housed two 35 ton capacity overhead cranes. Both shed and repair shop were built to Caledonian Railway standard designs being similar to Dundee, Aberdeen (Ferryhill) and Grangemouth. There were more than 200 locomotive here in 1924 but ten years later, the number was pruned to 144. However, by December 1947, the allocation had risen to 162 of which 61 were ex-Caledonian types. Coded 27A in 1935, Polmadie was recoded 66A by British Railways in January 1949. The depot closed to steam in May 1967 and became a diesel depot. All sign of the shed has now gone but the site is still used for stabling purposes.

*National Railway Museum*

*Plate 182:* An 'official' view of the completed works at the rear of Polmadie Shed, as seen in May 1930. The sand drying house, in the centre of the picture, was part of the new work and was demolished a few years after to be replaced by a Kelbus sand drying plant which was sited at the front of the shed. Behind the oil store can be seen a 50 ft. turntable which was left over from Caledonian days. The water tank above the repair shop held 112,000 gallons (500 tons) or enough for twenty eight fair-sized tenders.

*National Railway Museum*

*Plate 183:* Six years later, the rear yard at Polmadie had changed considerably with a new 70ft. vacuum-operated turntable now located on the site of the old sand furnace, replacing the 50ft. unit. Some years later, the 70ft. unit was resited at the southern end of the yard, some 700 yards from the shed.

*V. Forster Collection*

*Plate 184:* The new order had arrived with War Department locomotives in abundance, at Rose Grove in 1949, and only one ex-L&YR engine is on view. The coaling plant was a favourite vantage point for many photographers after it was built in 1936, and this view captures the atmosphere of a steam motive power depot on a weekend. On the left can be seen the roofless shed which, some twelve months later, had acquired a new concrete and glazed roof.

*A. George*

*Plate 185:* A 1935 view of Rose Grove before modernization had altered the yard layout. The shed had always housed freight locomotives together with only a handful of tank engines for passenger duties. Coded 24B by the LMS, after being code 23 in the L&YR list, it was again re-coded, in 1963, and became 10F.

*H. C. Casserley Collection*

*Plate 186:* Opened in 1899 by the Lancashire & Yorkshire Railway, Rose Grove engine shed was sited just to the west of Burnley. It had a six road 'northlight' shed, a standard coal stage and a 55ft. turntable. The shed roof was rebuilt as three separate sections over a period of ten years finally being completed in 1957 in the concrete and glazed style. This March 1968 view shows the general layout of the depot which has now been cleared completely since its closure in August 1968.

*A. Sommerfield*

*Plate 187:* The prospect of coaling their Ivatt 2-6-2T by hand, direct from the wagon on a warm day in May 1959, seems to have exhausted these two enginemen before they start. The shed is Seaton, after the fire which damaged part of the roof in April 1957. Opened in 1895, the wooden shed was constructed to house the Uppingham branch engine, a function it performed until 1961 when services on the branch were withdrawn.

*Brian Hilton*

*Plate 188:* At the Grouping, the LMS inherited three engine sheds at Sheffield, two ex-Midland sheds, Millhouses in the south of the city and Grimesthorpe in the heart of the industrial area, and this small ex-LNWR establishment at Nunnery, which was found to be surplus to requirements. Built in 1896, complete with a standard coaling stage, this four road shed was a sub-shed of Colwick, prior to 1922. It was open for less than thirty years, closing in July 1925. This official photograph, taken some two and a half years after closure, shows the shed being used for wagon repairs and storage, a fate which befell its parent shed in 1932.

*National Railway Museum*

*Plate 189:* The LTSR locomotive yard at Shoeburyness, around 1911, showing locomotives lined up at the coaling platform. Of particular interest are the coaling baskets stacked up and also the lack of cover for the coalman. It is no wonder that this depot was an early candidate for LMS modernization. The engine shed, seen in the background, had been constructed some three years previously. The two locomotives nearest to the camera, complete with coal bunker covers, are both Whitelegg 4-4-2 tanks, No. 47 *Stratford* and No. 80 *Thundersley*, the latter engine having now been preserved.

*A. G. Ellis*

*Plate 190:* Shoeburyness Shed, in 1934, with a visitor in the shape of Stanier 2-6-0 No. 13261 standing on No. 1 road. The recently built two road extension has the corrugated sheeting so common during this period. The destination boards which were carried on the ends of locomotives were a feature of this line as were the surburban tank engines that ran along it. Midland Railway property from 1912, Shoeburyness became 13D, in the 1935 shed LMS code list but, in February 1949, it came under Eastern Region control and picked up the code 33C, closing in June 1962 after the electrification of the ex-London, Tilbury & Southend lines.

*V. Forster Collection*

*Plate 191:* Shrewsbury LNWR shed, in 1901, with a fine array of 'Premier Line' motive power 'on shed'. This was one of the few 'northlight' type sheds to reach the 1960s without alteration and, when erected in 1877, it must have been built exceptionally well, as the shed was a busy establishment, with over forty locomotives allocated, for most of its life. Built nearby was the Great Western roundhouse and in front of that was a shed that the two companies shared for many years until the LNWR moved into this shed.

*OPC Collection*

*Plate 192:* Aspinall 0-6-0 No. 12141 was well away from its home ground when photographed at Shrewsbury in August 1933. Shed 30, as Shrewsbury was known, then acquired a number of these reliable engines from 1931 onwards and, by 1947, there were ten examples of ex-Lancashire & Yorkshire 0-6-0s on the books and when one was required for 'shopping' at Horwich, its place would be taken by another.

*W. L. Good*

*Plate 193:* The first day of 1968 and Shrewsbury Shed has finished with steam, having been officially closed, eight weeks before, to anything but diesels. The 70ft. turntable, installed in 1940, had been taken away and its pit was filling with water. Such was the end of the steam era when everything associated with that form of traction had a derelict unwanted aura about it.

*J. A. Sommerfield*

*Plate 194:* Southport ex-L&YR shed as seen around 1938. The six road dead end shed was of typical period design with a 'westernlight' roof. Yard facilities included a standard type coaling stage and, by this time, a 60ft. turntable had replaced a 50ft. unit. When this shed was opened in 1891 it replaced two smaller adjacent establishments of East Lancashire and West Lancashire origin, concentrating all the Southport locomotive department's interests under one roof. Under the LMS modernization scheme, this depot was planned to receive a mechanical coaling plant and a single skip ash plant but World War II intervened and the plans were never carried out. The shed roof, which was partly rebuilt in 1939, was completed by British Railways to the old LMS single pitch design.

*A. Sommerfield Collection*

*Plate 195:* The former West Lancashire Railway engine shed at Southport, in 1977, part of which was used as an electricity sub-station after its closure.

*J. A. Peden*

*Plate 196:* The ex-LNWR engine shed at Stafford, in March 1960. The LMS had altered the track layout during 1937, when the coaling and ash plants were erected just in front of what was a four road hipped roof shed which was demolished in the same year to make way for a 60ft. turntable. The six road shed was also a hipped roof affair until it was rebuilt in 1945/6. Just behind the 'Jinty', shunting on the left, can be seen the 32 bed lodging house, one of 42 such establishments spread about the LMS system and which disappeared with the end of steam. Coded 5C by both the LMS and British Railways, the depot closed in July 1965 but the shed was still standing in 1982.

*British Rail*

*Plate 197:* When the LMS handed over Stirling Engine Shed to British Railways, it was just 100 years old and much of the original shed was still standing. The only changes made during that century were the demolition of the arched doorways and alterations to the roof cladding. The four road through shed was sited just south of the station and was equipped with a single road coaling stage and a 52ft. turntable. A purpose-built fitting shop was erected as late as 1955 and prior to this date, all running repairs were done in the shed. The LMS had planned to build a new engine shed, complete with mechanical coal and ash facilities, but the plan, although revived by British Railways, was never implemented. In 1934, there were 44 locomotives allocated, all ex-Caledonian types, ranging from 4-6-0s to 0-4-4 tank engines. The allocation, on the eve of nationalization, was down to thirty two with three LMS 4F 0-6-0s joining the clan. This April 1959 view shows the mixed bag to be found here in British Railways' days. The shed closed on 13th June 1966.

*W. T. Stubbs*

*Plate 198:* The roundhouse at Stoke, as seen from the coaling plant, in September 1939. As can be seen, by this time, half of the roof had been taken down.

*A. G. Ellis*

*Plate 199:* A view looking from the refurbished section of the roundhouse at Stoke, in 1952, towards what remained of the original internal wall. Clearance for LMS standard tank engines was minimal. The roundhouse was rumoured to be a 'listed' building, but it was demolished during the 1970s.

*British Rail*

The ex-North Staffordshire Railway motive power depot at Stoke, was sited on both sides of the main lines at Stoke Junction. A roundhouse, built in the 1850s, stood on the west side of the line and on the east side was a straight shed built towards the end of the last century. The roundhouse was a circular shed of substantial construction which cost in excess of £17,000 when built. There were twenty four roads provided which included two entrance/exit roads. The 50ft. turntable was left open to the sky and each stabling road was entered through a brick archway. A 60 ton capacity overhead crane ran around the closed in section of the shed.

*Plate 200:* A pre-grouping scene at Stoke straight shed around 1912. In 1923, there were one hundred and twenty five locomotives allocated to this, the largest of the NSR sheds. In December 1947, there were ninety five engines allocated, of which just two were pre-grouping types; LNWR 'Cauliflower' 0-6-0s, Nos. 28442 and 28460. The remainder were LMS standard types and included thirty seven 2-6-4 tanks.

*Ron Dyer Collection*

*Plate 201:* A superb view, photographed from the newly-erected 150 ton capacity single bunker coaling plant at Stoke, in July 1936, showing the abundance of LMS-built locomotives, together with just a few ex-NSR examples. Coded shed 40, in the pre-1935 list, Stoke was coded 5D in the universal list; a code it kept until its closure in August 1967.

*British Rail*

*Plate 202:* The small complex of engine sheds at Stranraer was jointly established, in the 1870s, by the Caledonian and Glasgow & South Western railways to serve the seaport and was sited in the fork of the Stranraer Harbour and Stranraer to Portpatrick branches. Each company shedded about a dozen locomotives and the facilities were shared. These facilities included the workshops and a 50ft. turntable. The LMS saw fit to install a small 25 ton capacity coaling plant, in 1937, which was worked on the bucket hoist system with an overhead bunker. This plant was the first of its type and was called the 'Stranraer' and examples were erected at other depots on the LMS system. By December 1947, the allocation at Stranraer had dropped to only twelve locomotives, of which five were LMS 4-4-0s. In this August 1962 view, the depot was still busy handling some of the larger British Railways' passenger types including 'Clan' class Pacifics. The depot closed in 1966.

*K. Fairey*

*Plate 203:* St. Enoch, the former Glasgow & South Western Railway engine shed, stood just to the east of the station of the same name in the centre of Glasgow. Opened in 1884, facilities included a 50 ft. turntable and a coaling platform complete with a crane. In the pre-grouping period, forty locomotives were allocated and, when the shed closed in 1935, the residue of the allocation was sent to Corkerhill.

*W. A. Camwell*

*Plate 204:* A cleaner commences the task of polishing this LMS-built Caledonian-designed 0-4-4T outside St. Enoch Shed in September 1934. Even at this early date, only seven ex-G&SWR engines remained on the books out of the twenty nine locomotives which were allocated.

*W. L. Good*

*Plate 205:* Ex-G&SWR Manson 275 class 0-6-0T No. 16109 carries out shed pilot duties at St. Enoch Depot in 1931. The transverse hipped roof pitches of the shed were quite a departure from previous G&SWR roof designs. The coaling crane control cabin can be seen on the left, and one of the signal gantries controlling main line movements to and from the nearby terminus dominates the top of the picture.

*G. Coltas*

*Plate 206:* The Garnkirk & Glasgow Railway opened this engine shed at St. Rollox in the early 1830s and it lasted, for locomotive stabling purposes, until 1847 after which it was taken over by the Permanent Way Department. The unusual thing about this shed was the fact that living accommodation was built, from the outset, above the shed. Would it have been classed as a 'garage' shed if it had been open in 1935?

*National Railway Museum*

*Plate 207:* Located at the junction of the Somerset & Dorset and ex-London & South Western main lines, Templecombe was chosen as the site for an engine shed, in the 1880s, and this timber building was all that remained of the original shed by 1951. The new two road shed is visible in the background. One of the S & D route's famous 2-8-0s is drawing up to the coaling crane, which is a small petrol driven mobile crane sitting on top of a pile of sleepers. The turntable was one of the unbalanced manual types where positioning of the locomotive was all important.

*A. R. Goult*

*Plate 208:*    There is very little room left on this day in July 1957, when Templecombe, the new shed now complete, offers every available space to a mixed bag of motive power. In 1935, with the line now under full LMS control, this depot was coded 22D and in British Railways' days was transferred to Southern Region control and later, to Western Region control together with the other ex-S&D engine sheds.

*K. Fairey*

*Plate 209:*    Thurso was the most northerly engine shed in the British Isles and, befitting of such an outpost, it had spartan servicing facilities with a coaling platform and a 45 ft. turntable. The shed was built in 1874 from local stone, the Highland Railway always making use of what was easily available. Extension rails were fitted to the turntable at some time before 1945 to increase the diameter to 52 ft. The shed was closed when steam was banished from the far north of Scotland in 1962.

*Brian Hilton*

*Plate 210:* Toton was one of the largest motive power depots on the LMS in terms of both size and allocation. The first engine shed was built at Toton in the 1850s but was superseded by three roundhouses built, in 1870, 1873 and 1900, by the Midland Railway to serve the vast coal traffic from the East Midlands pits. All three roundhouses survived into LMS and later British Railways' ownership, the two oldest sheds receiving new roofs when British Railways took over. This 1932 view, taken from the top of the new coaling plant, shows the new double skip ash disposal plant with a Beyer-Garratt locomotive going through the servicing procedure. To the left of the shed is the north yard of Toton Sidings, where empty wagons await their journey back to the collieries.

*V. Forster Collection*

*Plate 211:* Toton coaling stage being dismantled, in 1930, to make way for the new mechanical coaling plant. During alterations such as these, alternative coaling arrangements had to be made at certain depots whereby a timber coaling shelter would be erected. This, in some cases, could be a large structure, with raised coaling roads, built up on piles of old sleepers.

*National Railway Museum*

*Plate 212:* Toton, in 1961, with many of the depot's 4F 0-6-0 allocation 'on shed'. At the Grouping, Midland shed 17, as Toton was then coded, had one hundred and forty two 0-6-0s out of its total allocation of one hundred and eighty locomotives. By 31st December 1947, the allocation comprised seventy three 0-6-0s, of 3F and 4F power class, fifty six Stanier 8Fs, twenty three Beyer-Garratts, eight 0-6-0 tank engines, six diesel shunters, an ex-MR 4-4-0, No. 526 and a solitary 'Black 5', No. 4829. The shed code was 18A, from 1935 onwards, but changed to 16A in September 1963. Two years later steam was all but finished when a new diesel depot, claimed to be the largest in Europe, and built alongside the roundhouses, was brought into use to service a 200+ fleet of diesel locomotives. The old steam sheds were demolished shortly afterwards.

*A. George*

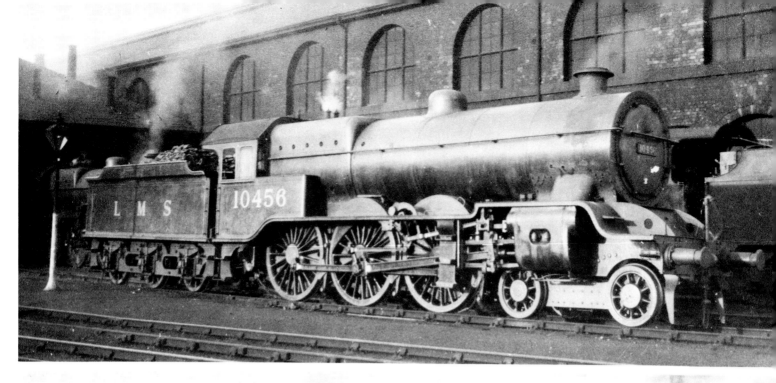

*Plates 213 & 214:*   Carlisle (Upperby) always had the best available motive power for working the heavy West Coast Main Line passenger trains, as these two 1930s' scenes show. The first view, taken about 1930, shows LMS-built 'Dreadnought', No. 10456 standing outside the eleven road shed. There were a number of these locomotives used on the WCML, the majority of which were allocated to Upperby. This particular locomotive was rebuilt in 1926 as a compound and was the only member of the class to be converted in this manner. 'Royal Scots' were soon allocated, after their introduction in 1927, and in May 1933, No. 6137 *Vesta,* renamed *The Prince of Wales's Volunteers (South Lancashire)* in 1936, looking resplendent outside the dilapidated shed, is made ready by its driver for the journey south. Eventually, of course, the Stanier Pacifics took over the principal express workings. The shed was replaced by a large concrete roundhouse, similar to the Leicester roundhouse, but closure came in December 1966 some years after the big engines had given way to new forms of traction.

*M Bentley Collection and V. Forster*

*Plate 215:* An undated photograph of Uttoxeter, which was one of the last ex-North Staffordshire Railway engine sheds to close. Opened in 1900 in the triangle formed by the Burton, Leek and Stoke lines, this 'northlight' type shed replaced an earlier establishment sited near Pinfold Crossing. A timber-built coaling stage was supplied but the need for a turntable was discarded in favour of using the adjacent triangle. Coded 5F in 1935, this was one of the few depots to keep its original code up to its closure in December 1964.

*A. G. Ellis*

*Plate 216:* A Stanier 2-6-4T, complete with electrification warning flashes, emerges from the coal stage ready for its next turn, during the last years of the shed's existence. The allocation of Uttoxeter on the last day of the LMS consisted of 4F 0-6-0s Nos. 4307 and 4504, 4P 2-6-4Ts Nos. 2358, 2363 and 2468 and 3P 2-6-2Ts Nos. 85, 86 and 156.

*A. Sommerfield*

*Plates 217 & 218:* Two interior scenes that could be found at any motive power depot during the steam era. The first view shows the mess room and the other photograph portrays a typical general office. Both views were recorded at the ex-LNWR shed at Walsall in 1952.

*British Rail*

*Plate 219:* An undated photograph of Wellingborough taken during the latter part of the LMS period with a party, of what were probably white-coated officials, inspecting the premises. The shed in view is No. 1, with No. 2 out of picture to the right. In the distance can be seen the ash and coal plants, whilst the shed on the right was the Beyer-Garratt stabling shed and, prior to this, it was the depot's coaling shed.

*Author's Collection*

*Plate 220:* With the water softening plant casting a shadow over the firebox of Beyer-Garratt locomotive No. 4995 (later No. 7995), the large locomotive stands amongst the attractive shrubbery at the rear of No. 1 shed at Wellingborough, in September 1933. These locomotives were part of the everyday scene at this depot from their introduction until their withdrawal. The main function of the depot was to provide freight engines for Midland main line trains but there were also three 4-4-0s on the allocation, at the end of 1947, for working passenger trains. The other seventy three locomotives shedded here at this time included thirty six Stanier 2-8-0s and eight ex-LNWR 0-8-0s.

*H. C. Casserley*

*Plate 221:*    The ex-Caledonian Railway engine shed at Wemyss Bay must be the ideal location for modelling, with the 43 ft. turntable feeding the single road shed which is complete with advertisements. This tiny depot closed just before World War II. In the background, completing this attractive scene, can be seen the pier from where railway steamers sailed, mainly to Rothesay.

*W. A. Camwell*

*Plate 222:*    Stanier 5MT, No. 44991, of Inverness (60A), stands outside Wick Shed, in August 1959, in company with the Cowans Sheldon 15 ton capacity steam breakdown crane of G & S W R 1893 vintage. Opened in 1874 by the Highland Railway, Wick managed to retain its original shed building until closure in 1962. The line on the right led to the 55 ft. turntable.

*P. Tatlow*

*Plate 223:* Widnes (Tanhouse Lane) was erected around 1880 with funds provided by the Cheshire Lines Committee. Both the Midland Railway and Manchester, Sheffield & Lincolnshire Railway stabled locomotives here. Although the Midland only had one resident 0-6-0T engine here, other locomotives passed through, bringing or taking freight from the town. This June 1939 view, has 'Jinty' No. 7464 posing together with interested parties, outside the two road shed. The shed closed in 1956 after which the larger ex-LNWR depot in the district took over the remaining duties.

*Ron Dyer Collection*

*Plate 224:* A somewhat rare photograph of the Lancashire & Yorkshire Railway engine shed at Wigan (Pagefield) in 1891. Opened in 1878, to serve the growing coal traffic around the Wigan area, the shed had an equal pitch 'westernlight' roof and a coal stage was provided in the yard. By the 1890s, both the shed and yard were suffering from local mining subsidence. L&YR minutes, that are available, do not elaborate on the subsidence menace and mention is made only of repairs etc. However, by 1893, events must have become desperate as a new site was sought away from Pagefield and, in 1896, a new fourteen road shed, built mainly of timber, with an unusually high 'northlight' roof, was erected 700 yards to the east, on the opposite side of the line. Timber uprights took the place of the usual cast-iron columns as roof supports at the new shed, and the office accommodation was built on raised foundations. All these precautions enabled filling to take place in the future if subsidence struck again. Some sources stated that the need for the new shed was due to the lack of room for expansion at Pagefield but, looking at plans and, indeed, this photograph, room for extra accommodation was available and it seems strange to move from a substantial brick-built and comparitively new shed, into a timber structure.

*Revd. W. A. Wickham*

*Plate 225:*   The timber-built ex-L&YR engine shed at Wigan, as seen in September 1962. Much of the original fourteen road shed had been taken down by this time and only two roads retained the original length roof section, whilst six roads were covered by only half the shed and the rest were open to the elements; No. 14 road had been taken up completely. From an allocation of seventy eight locomotives in 1922, a steady decline set in during the LMS period reducing to fifty nine engines by 1934 and only thirty nine engines by December 1947. These Stanier 2-6-2 and 2-6-4 tank locomotives are stored on No. 9 road awaiting removal to a Scottish scrap merchant. Wigan Central, as it was then known, played host to many stored and withdrawn steam locomotives, in the 1960s, even after closure in April 1964. All trace of the depot is now gone.

*A. George*

*Plate 226:*   The ex-Caledonian shed at Yoker provided motive power for the various goods yards on the north bank of the River Clyde. As a sub-shed of Dawsholm, the depot had a timber coaling stage and a 60ft. turntable, both necessary for servicing the many visiting goods engines. During Caledonian days, the shed was known as Rothesay Dock Engine Shed and tank engines were its usual residents as the October 1933 allocation lists show. These included 0-6-0Ts Nos. 16162, 16170, 16171, 16238 and 16295, and 0-4-0 saddle tanks Nos. 16010 and 16039. The depot closed to steam in 1964 and diesel shunters can still be found stabled around the remains of the shed at weekends.

*W. T. Stubbs*

# CLOSED, SOLD, DERELICT AND DEMOLITION   How the end came and went

*Plate 227:* Forres on 22nd June 1963, roofless and derelict after twelve months out of use. One noticeable feature of the building is the intact windows which is very unusual. Perhaps the location of this shed has something to do with this.

*W. T. Stubbs*

*Plate 228:* Looking nearly as good as new, is the ex-Caledonian shed at Callander, photographed in September 1959, thirty years after its closure.

*W. T. Stubbs*

*Plate 229:* The ex-LNWR stone-built shed at Craven Arms, as seen in 1974, ten years after its closure.

*D. J. Clarke*

*Plate 230:* Many engine sheds, closed before or after the Grouping, found a new lease of life as wagon repair shops and the Glasgow & South Western Railway shed at Carlisle (Currock Junction) was one such shed, as this May 1963 view shows. The shed was built in 1896 to house about forty G & S W R locomotives, then stationed at Carlisle, but, in June 1924, all the engines and staff were transferred to the ex-Caledonian shed at Kingmoor and the Currock Junction shed, being in such good condition, took on its new role. On the left of the photograph can be seen the site of the former Maryport & Carlisle engine shed, with the water tower still intact.

*D. F. Tee*

*Plate 231 (below):* Coalville, on 12th May 1968. With the tracks taken up and the buildings empty, the former Midland Railway engine shed awaits the demolition gang. Opened in 1890, the three road shed was of standard M R straight shed design and had replaced a smaller shed dating back to the early days of the Midland Railway. Closure took place on 4th October 1965 and demolition took place in August 1969.

*D. F. Tee*

*Plate 232:*   Closed in June 1961, as a result of dieselization of the Manchester route, Macclesfield Shed had been the home of tank engines for 112 years. Although built and owned by the North Staffordshire Railway, access to the site was gained over LNWR metals. The shed building remained in its original condition until the LMS fitted a new concrete roof in the early 1930s. The site is now cleared and any clue that an engine shed once stood here is impossible to find.

*Ron Dyer*

*Plate 233:*   Ellesmere Port was closed, by the LNWR, in 1921 and was rented out to the Manchester Ship Canal Co. not long afterwards for use of their locomotives which were shunting the area. On this dull day, in July 1961, the timber 'northlight' shed was still giving good service, although its surroundings were, by this time, somewhat untidy. Ten years later, the shed, once again redundant, was still standing.

*W. T. Stubbs*

*Plate 234:* The type of roof structure adopted by British Railways in its early years was a virtual copy of the design used by the LMS from the early 1940s, and in this 1970 view of Goole, only the square chimney vents give away the fact that the shed was rebuilt in 1950 and not by the LMS. Prior to its rebuilding, Goole was topped by a 'northlight' roof which dated from the opening of the shed in 1889. The structure is reminiscent of the Hornby 'Dublo' shed kit which was produced some years ago. *J. A. Sommerfield*

*Plate 235:* The former LNWR engine shed at Netherfield & Colwick, photographed in May 1965, nearly thirty three years after closure, remarkably intact and used by a light engineering concern. After closure, the shed was used for some years as a wagon repair shop before passing into private use.

*W. T. Stubbs*

Plate 236: Preston ex-LNWR shed after closure, in September 1961, was used for the storage of withdrawn locomotives from other depots. An ex-LMS 'Patriot', having just arrived from Carnforth, stands beneath the remains of the shed roof, in the part of the shed that suffered during the terrible fire of 1960.

*A. George*

Plate 237: No. 2 shed at Wellingborough was taken over by a private company in the late 1960s, and was one of a number of ex-Midland Railway 'square' roundhouses that passed into private ownership and gained a new lease of life. This was surely a tribute to their design. This particular shed was built in 1872 and served steam locomotives until 1966. The No. 1 shed at Wellingborough was built some five years before this building and was demolished in 1964 to make way for a diesel servicing depot.

*British Rail*

*Plate 238:*  The ex-Midland Railway engine shed at Colne, in the course of demolition in 1936, only weeks after closure. This tiny two road shed, built sometime during the 1870s, had replaced what was probably a wooden building dating from days when the Midland Railway had entered North-East Lancashire. Until 1900, the L&YR had stabled engines here, usually outnumbering the MR stud by three to one, but, in that year, they moved to a new shed sited to the south of Colne Station. Ironically, the L&YR shed also closed in 1936 and stood derelict for many years before demolition took place.

*W. A. Camwell*

*Plate 239:*  The ex-LNWR shed at Swansea, photographed in October 1962, just over three years after closure. Like most of the 'northlight' sheds erected by this company the roof did not fair too well against the ravages of smoke and weather.

*W. T. Stubbs*

# A SELECTION OF RESIDENTS

*Plate 240:* Webb 0-6-2T No. 7763, complete with a 'not to be moved' sign, awaits attention at the fitter's bench inside Bletchley Shed, in 1938.

*G. Coltas*

*Plate 241:* Weighing in at a mere 23 tons, and being dwarfed by its stablemates, this ex-MR saddle tank sports both its new BR number and its freshly-painted LMS lettering, in September 1948, in Derby Shed yard.

*W. Potter*

*Plate 242:* A Midland-derived LMS Standard 4F 0-6-0, No. 4166, simmers in the yard at Saltley, circa 1935. The bulk of the former Midland Railway shed's allocation was made up of these reliable 0-6-0s.

*W. L. Good*

*Plate 243:* Stanier Mogul No. 13268 is prepared for the road, alongside Willesden coaling plant, in April 1934.

*W. L. Good*

*Plate 244:* Standing in the frost-laden atmosphere, Ivatt 2-6-0 No. 46480 bears witness to the harsh winters experienced at Buxton Shed, in this January 1963 view.

*G. Coltas*

*Plate 245:* 'Whale' 4F 4-6-0 No. 8786 of Patricroft, undergoes repair inside Springs Branch (Wigan) Depot in July 1936.

*W. Potter*

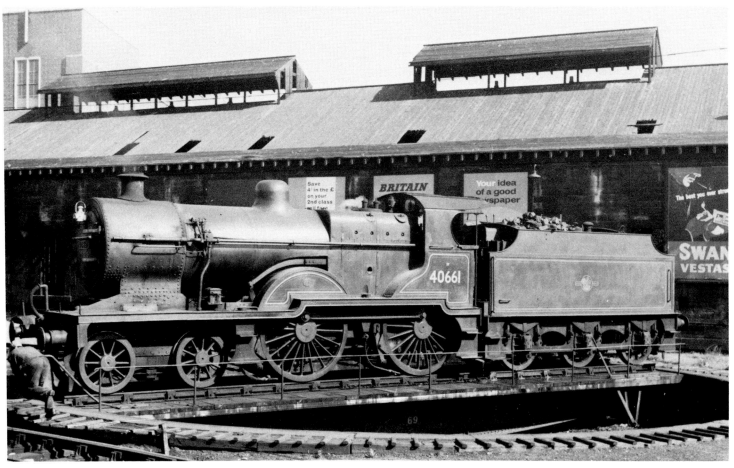

*Plate 246:* The fireman of LMS-built 4-4-0 No. 40661 slowly turns his engine on the 50 ft. turntable which is situated next to the former G&SWR shed at Kilmarnock.

*V. Forster*

*Plate 247:* On shed a steam loco-motive seemed almost demure, compared with the controlled power and violence of which it was capable, once unleashed. Aspinall 2-4-2T No. 10852, stand-ing on a Sunday morning in May 1938 at Wakefield Shed, was no exception.

*W. L. Good*

*Plate 248:* Ex-LTSR 2P No. 2096, far from its home ground, is seen here in No. 1 shed at Nottingham. This, and other members of its class, was resident at this former MR shed for many years, having been displaced from the LTS section by the Stanier 2-6-4 three cylinder tank engines.

*W. Potter*

*Plate 249:* The graceful lines of the 'Jubilees' are well depicted in this view of No. 5701 *Conqueror* at its home shed, Newton Heath, in April 1939.

*W. Potter*

*Plate 250:* Looking as dilapidated as its surroundings, No. 1661, an ex-MR Johnson 1F 0-6-0T, stands beneath the almost non-existent roof of No. 1 roundhouse at Kentish Town.

*W. Potter*

*Plate 251:* A running repair is carried out on No. 17646, an ex-CR McIntosh 30 class 0-6-0, at Polmadie in 1934. Inside cylinder locomotives presented problems to fitters, especially if a pit was not available.

*W. L. Good*

*Plate 252:* Cricklewood, on 23rd May 1969. Demolition was the fate of most steam engine sheds and here the contractors' work is almost complete. Opened in 1882, Cricklewood, or Child's Hill as it was then known, was a typical Midland establishment and by 1893 it consisted of two 'square' roundhouses, housing mainly freight and shunting locomotives that served the adjacent Brent Sidings. British Railways rebuilt the two sheds in the early 1950s, using precast concrete segments, but, in December 1964, the depot closed to steam and a few years later was also vacated by diesel traction to await its fate.

*British Rail*

# Acknowledgements

As mentioned in the introduction, it was the men behind the cameras who made this book possible and also those people who allowed me access to their own collections. Listed below are individuals I would like to thank and also organizations that have helped with reasearch. My apologies are extended to anyone omitted.

Alex Appleton
Roy Anderson
Mike Bentley
Bill Camwell
H. C. Casserley
David Clarke
Gordon Coltas
W. D. Cooper
Eddie Dixon
Ron Dyer
John Edgington
The late A. G. Ellis
Bob Essery
Ken Fairey
Jimmy Fishwick
Vic Forster
Greg Fox
Alec George
A. R. Goult
Brian Hilton
Bernard Matthews
George McArthur
Jim Peden
Bill Potter
Tim Shuttleworth
Alan Sommerfield
Bill Stubbs
Peter Tatlow
David Tee
Nelson Twells

British Railways
LMS Society
L & Y R Society
National Railway Museum
Photomatic